A Gathering
of
Our Days

AUDRAIN
COUNTY
MISSOURI

© CARTOGRAPHIC WORKS, 1997

A Gathering
of
Our Days

Selected Writings on the History of
Mexico and Audrain County, Missouri

by Leta Hodge

Audrain County Historical Society
Mexico, Missouri
1997

ISBN 0-9646625-9-0   14.95

Cover photograph by Brett Dufur.
Author photograph by Brett Dufur.

Cartographer: Lawrence "Ted" Twenter, Cartographic Works, Columbia, Missouri, USA
Designers and Publishers: Brian Beatte & Brett Dufur—Pebble Publishing, Columbia, Missouri, USA
Printer and Binder: Ovid Bell Press, Fulton, Missouri, USA
Typefaces: Caslon Openface BT & Times New Roman

For the
People of Audrain County

Especially
Susan, Rebecca, Elizabeth
and
Edward

Contents

VIII

The Best Community in the Entire Middle West

IX

With Indomitable Spirit

X

Notes and Index

Acknowledgments

$\mathbb{R}$esearch for a history such as this involves the help of many. My thanks go to the following institutions:

The Audrain County Historical Society, its officers and directors, its staff and its membership. Their aid and support provided me with access to a major source of material and information. During my work there—for some months in the mid-1960s and again as director from 1980 to 1990— I had the opportunity to seek out and absorb the essence of our local history; I am most grateful. My thanks go as well to the many members who kindly encouraged my initial efforts in writing the county's story.

The *Mexico Ledger*, in particular Robert M. White and James E. Sterner, for so graciously allowing me access to its files and records.

The Mexico-Audrain Library, particularly Christal Bruner and Violet Lierheimer, for help with microfilm and obtaining material from other libraries.

The Audrain County Recorder's Office and Virginia Pehle for aid in finding and copying appropriate material.

The Mexico Board of Education, particularly Frances Sutton, secretary, for making available school records.

My appreciation goes also to many individuals who have, over the years, deepened my understanding of the county. Some have described people, events and places, pointed out items of importance and, through countless conversations, shared their memories. Others have loaned me related material, given suggestions, and checked my facts. While I hesitate to list any for fear of omitting someone, the following were especially generous; though many are no longer with us, I wish to express my sincere gratitude to each:

Eugene Affolter, Betty L. Baker, Elma Lee Barnes, Edna Bickley, Janet Botkins, Virginia E. Botts, Louis E. Boyes, Bradford Brett, Alan Coatsworth, George Craddock, Roy Creasey, Mary Frances Crews, Effie L. Davis, Frank B. Edwards, Dr. H. Peter Ekern, Gene Gallagher, Tim Hagan, L. B. Hawthorne, Alfred Hicks, Clara Kaiser, Maurice Kemp, Frank Kent, Geraldine Lewis, Kathryn Locke, Hudson Long, Ralph Luckaman, Martha Dent Mason, Robert E. McIntosh, Warren O. McIntyre, Dr. H. I. Nesheim, Janet B. Nesheim, Harriet Pasqueth, Clarence Ray, G. Andy Runge, Elenore Schewe, Dale Schnarre, Essielee Playter Snook, Miriam Spicer, Martha Green Staley, Colonel C. R. Stribling Jr., Colonel Charles R. Stribling III, Ruth Cauthorn Stribling, Carleton Larsen Toalson, Martha Tuepker and Frank P. Wilfley.

A special word of thanks is given to Grazia R. Svokos who has served as advisor, for her suggestions, expertise and patient understanding.

Every effort has been made to avoid errors. Any mistakes are, of course, fully the responsibility of the author.

Preface

As a child I once stood in the elegant library of an old Virginia mansion and gazed with curiosity at a clouded jar into which someone had stuffed what looked like a dirty, bloody old rag. Carefully taking the jar from the shelf, my mother's friend explained that it held the handkerchief used by her grandfather to wash the wounds of the Confederate General Stonewall Jackson as he lay dying down by the river.

I was fascinated.

I knew nothing about what she called "the War," much less Stonewall Jackson. But I sensed that there was something important about this, and that whatever it was somehow affected this lady's personality and the way we all lived. From then on, though at first I realized it only dimly, a fascination with history became a part of my life.

Its attraction grew stronger as I studied history at college, taught it in high school and pursued graduate studies on political, social and cultural America. Through historical research and interpretation I began to understand how the present rests upon the past and the future derives its character from what has gone before.

When I moved to Mexico in 1961 the fascination deepened. What kind of past did this county called Audrain have? What made it prosper? Who were its people? What was its history?

As I worked for the Audrain County Historical Society over the years I began to find some of the answers. Courthouse records and county histories supplied facts and dates. Older people talked about families, buildings, events and individuals now long gone. Old photographs, scrapbooks, letters, a diary, newspaper clippings—all held clues to the county's past.

Gradually her history took shape. Applying academic standards to all I found, I connected the county to the history of Missouri and the history of the United States. Average in so many ways, Audrain County was also unique.

Her past formed an interesting story. Schoolchildren, visitors, newcomers curious about their adopted home, and even longtime residents aware of the passing years could, I felt, benefit from a record of the county's struggles and accomplishments told in narrative form.

As director of the historical society I began a series of short articles for its newsletter depicting various aspects of the county's past. They were well received, prompting plans for a collection of these mini-histories.

For this work, since these separate, more focused articles appealed to both casual readers and those well grounded in history, I have chosen to remain with that format. My aim is not a sweeping story of the county from early times to the present, nor a comprehensive history covering all phases of her development. Instead, I am presenting her past in short, independent narratives intended to stand alone but also to relate to her overall history.

Gathered here are selections covering Audrain's most outstanding and impressive days, as well as pieces describing some less noteworthy but equally engaging moments of her past. For each section a topic was selected to be explored as to facts, general interest, and significance to the county. Earlier articles were revised and expanded, new ones written, and closer attention given to historical import. Where possible they have been placed in appropriate chronological order.

In an effort to limit the size of the book, choices had to be made and some topics omitted. I regret, for instance, that space could not be given to each town and community in the county. Emphasis was placed on Mexico, the largest, and as the county seat symbolic of all.

The people of Mexico and Audrain have been good to me and mine. Though not a native, perhaps I dared offer this effort in appreciation of their welcome, their acceptance and their friendship. May it encourage in its readers a sense of pride and affection for this place that is home.

In this spirit I present the following history of Audrain County.

A Gathering
of
Our Days

I

Her Grand and Beautiful Prairie

1

Whittling Down the Wilderness

The land, of course, was always here, with its fire clay soil and fertile tallgrass prairie. But only in the 1830s was it civilized and bound into the political entity known as Audrain County. Old maps show it as a tiny spot lost in a western wilderness that had no boundaries and no name. As the course of history whittled down the wilderness, Audrain's specific area took shape and many a hopeful pioneer carved out his own particular portion of her land.

The area that would one day be called Audrain covered 680 square miles of land—rich land, whose wealth in the beginning was not readily apparent. Its soil in some places appeared yellowish-gray, thick and hard like clay, its sod in others, tough and compact, with grass growing "taller than a man on horseback."

From the ridgeline of higher ground that crossed it, small streams flowed northward into the Salt River and the Mississippi and southward into the Loutre and the Missouri. Across its hilly central section groves of cottonwood, oak and hickory trees clustered around creek banks. Toward the east and north, covering three-fourths of the future county, stretched her "grand and beautiful prairie."

Since time untold this stretch of treeless tallgrass prairie had marked the southern edge of a glacier that once curved down into Missouri, leaving behind rich fertile soil. Early settlers, baffled by this sea of tall waving grass, stood in awe of the prairie. Some, entranced by its blazing light, profusion of wildflowers and vast "swards of green" reaching unbroken to the horizon, felt immediately at home. Others lamented the "lonesome, windy, grassy place" and cringed from its relentless sun and monotonous, never-ending grass. Those who settled Audrain land, cultivating first the more familiar timbered tracts, learned only gradually to tame the grassland that "fell and rose and swayed again like the restless billows of the ocean."

Long before the first settler came to the land around the Salt River's South Fork, Indians wandered across it. Mainly the Missouri and Osage tribes, they left no trace of any permanent presence in the area. Later the Sauk, the Fox and the Pottowattomie hunted across it and sometimes camped along its streams.

During the 1600s Audrain's land lay in the French colonial empire that extended across the vast interior of the North American continent. A century later the land west of the Mississippi was dominated by Spain. In 1800 the Emperor Napoleon claimed it again for France—and decided to sell it. It became American in 1803 when President Thomas Jefferson paid France 15 million dollars for the Louisiana Purchase, including the 440,000 acres that one day would be Audrain.

Like a carpenter splitting a big piece of wood into desired objects, the national government in time carved the five hundred million acres known as Louisiana into smaller sections that were gradually settled and organized. When the Territory of Missouri was cut out in 1812, at first only a few counties were formed, each to include in its jurisdiction all unorganized land bordering on its west; Audrain's land fell into a large St. Charles County. As more people settled St. Charles, its smaller, permanent boundaries were drawn. A piece of the future Audrain then fell into a large Howard County, with the rest submerged in the changing boundaries of Ralls and Pike.

By the time Missouri became a state in 1821, settlers in its northeast section had set up counties along the Missouri and Mississippi Rivers, with a few claiming land north of the Salt. The rough triangle of unsettled land between would gradually give way to additional counties, leaving in the center a pocket of wilderness that included Audrain.

State legislators examining the map of Missouri ten years later found that pocket of wilderness still sparsely settled. Now bound by Pike, Ralls, Montgomery, Callaway, Boone and the recently established Monroe Counties it, too, would one day merit representation and its own government. Therefore in 1831 state legislators drew the outlines of a "contemplated county" that, until enough people settled it, would be "attached to" and within the jurisdiction of the surrounding counties. They selected for the proposed county the name Audrain.

The county of Audrain that finally emerged out of the vastness of the West was officially organized in 1836, the fifty-second in the state of Missouri. Settlers straggled into its shrinking wilderness, undaunted by its difficulties and trusting in the goodness of its land.

2

What's in Our Names?

Mexico—like Shakespeare's rose—by any other name would smell as sweet, and Audrain County, whatever its name, would still be home. But why these particular names, these "handles for posterity"?

The question of a name for the contemplated county they had outlined in the northeast wilderness of the state brought an immediate response from the 1831 Missouri legislature. Rejecting suggestions of *Union* and *Ioway,* members followed their customary pattern of naming counties for famous Americans and prominent Missourians. From Jefferson, Franklin and Jackson to Howard, Boone and Wayne, the state had honored many individuals in this way. Now, in tribute to a newly elected colleague who had recently died, into these roughly drawn boundary lines they sketched the name Audrain.

James H. Audrain, a son of Peter Audrain, French immigrant to America, had been born in 1782 in Pennsylvania. Following his father west as a young man, he for a time engaged in merchandising in Indiana, then moved to Kentucky, and in 1809 crossed the Mississippi to St. Louis. Described as "a man of nerve and enterprise," during the War of 1812 he was commissioned a Captain of Volunteers, a position also referred to as "captain of a company of spies," and served as captain of a company of U.S. Rangers—service that earned him the lifelong title of Colonel. After the war he settled in St. Charles County, where he built a mill and a distillery, operated an inn and gained local acclaim by winning a ten-dollar bet for carrying, by himself and in one trip, eight bushels of wheat up three

7

flights of stairs. In 1830 he was elected to the Missouri legislature from St. Charles but died in November of 1831, highly esteemed by his colleagues, who gave his name to the new contemplated county. After five years Missouri would formally add to its current roster of local governing bodies, the county of Audrain.

By the spring of 1836 Audrain settlers were anticipating the county's official organization. With this in mind two pioneer realtors, James H. Smith and the Reverend Robert C. Mansfield, were studying an area described as the northeast quarter of Section 26, Township 51, Range 9 West, located almost exactly in the middle of the proposed county. Near "the prongs of Davis Fork and Beaver Dam creeks," and covered with grass, a few bushes and some trees, it appeared the perfect spot for the county seat. Soon they were buying land and outlining lots for a proposed town to be named Mexico.

The new Missouri town owed the origin of its name to the current zeal over Texas, then a part of the country of Mexico. At that time the Missouri frontier was alive with tales of Texas, whose settlers were seeking independence and who had recently suffered a massacre at the Alamo. Many pioneers were headed for this area to claim land and make their fortunes. Two versions of the name's origin, both related to these events, have survived the years. One refers to a tavern sign reading "To Mexico," directing travelers to a trail toward the southwest. The more valid explanation, however, comes from George Robertson, a county historian writing in 1913 and citing William Mansfield, a son of the founder, as his source. They, writes Robertson,

> gave the town the name of Mexico, in recognition of the excitement at that time in this state over the growing controversy between Mexico and the United States concerning the independence of Texas. These proprietors thought that the note of the name would bring popularity to the town.

The Audrain founders were, indeed, confident that the reports of great wealth to be gained in Texas and the enthusiasm surrounding that southwest utopia would bring their new town prosperity and "popularity." The name of Mexico also no doubt seemed appropriate in a state already dotted with towns reminding people of exotic faraway places—Paris, New London, Troy and New Madrid, among others. Word slowly spread of the proposed prairie village of Mexico.

On April 23, 1836, Mansfield and Smith filed their plat for the town of Mexico and a few months later it was duly selected as the county seat.

Someone at the legislature mistakenly recorded it as New Mexico in the first records, but that error was quickly corrected, and the business of the county of Audrain proceeded at its county seat of Mexico.

In the years that followed, the smell of corn, horses and brick dust—and of steam engines, shoes and soybeans, offices, stores and roses—would mingle with the sweet smell of success to engender for those calling them home a high regard for the names of Mexico and Audrain.

STATE OF MISSOURI 1821

3

The Frontier's Diabolic Song

The contemplated county of Audrain was slow to be settled, and with good reason. Wrote one early historian:

> The territory which forms Audrain County up to 1837 was known as the "Salt River Region," and not even Hades with all its horrors was more uninviting to the timid female than a home within its borders. . . . Its primeval stillness was broken only by the hideous howl of the wolf, or the hair-raising whoop of the Sac or the Pottowattomie.

Settlers who ventured into her wilderness to grapple with her perils did so with courage, a capacity for hard work and a confidence born of self-reliance.

The first people other than Indians known to set foot in Audrain, around 1812, were five men from the Loutre Island settlement southeast of Audrain in pursuit of a band of Pottowattomies who had stolen their horses. When night fell they found themselves in "the Grand Prairie Country," where they set up camp near a small stream and deer lick. Thinking themselves unseen by the Indians they posted no guard, or else he failed in his duty, for the Indians fired on them while they were asleep, killing three and wounding a fourth. The fifth escaped and made his way back home, as eventually did the wounded man, carrying the sad story. A few years later the skulls of the slain men were found on the banks of the stream, which early settlers then named Skull Lick.

Although Indians were no longer a problem by 1820, prospective settlers eyeing Audrain land faced two other obstacles: no navigable rivers and no roads. The Salt River's South Fork, unlike its other branches, offered no help to settlers moving upstream. For years the only roads in the entire northeast region were the Boonslick Road, running from St. Charles west through Montgomery and Callaway Counties to Boonslick, and a rough trail from Boone County northeast toward Paris and on toward Palmyra— trails forty and fifty miles from Audrain. As elsewhere on the frontier, the first to wander into this isolated wilderness, paving the way for a second wave of farmers who would settle permanently, were hunters and trappers.

One of these wandering trappers—the first known to live, though briefly, on Audrain land, building along the banks of a creek a crude shelter for himself, his horse and his dogs—was a "misanthropic old Englishman" named Robert Littleby. Selecting his quarry from the elk, deer, beaver, otter, mink, raccoon, muskrat and occasional panther then roaming the Audrain wilds, he sold his "furs and peltries" in St. Charles. Known to be here in 1816, Littleby had moved on by 1822, leaving behind his recipe for curing meat—soak it one week in a strong concoction of lye—and his name, which soon became attached to the creek.

The first known settler to build a cabin and begin to farm in the county, probably in 1821, was an intrepid pioneer named Benjamin Young. Born in North Carolina, Young was raised by Indians and had married an Indian. Early historians record the following tale:

> In the same county there lived a woman named Mary Ring, who was captivated by Benjamin's prepossessing appearance, and proposed matrimony to him. He frankly told her that he was already married to the squaw, but had no desire to see her carried to an untimely grave from the effects of a broken heart, and if she would whip the squaw she might take him. She accepted the proposition, "cleaned out" the squaw and claimed her reward. Young was not the man to "go back" on his word, so he dismissed the squaw and married the white woman.

The two set out for the frontier, she and all their worldly goods on a pony and he on foot. They stopped first in Kentucky, then in Missouri's Howard County, and finally in north-central Audrain. Here they settled down by a small stream soon to be known as Young's Creek.

Only a few details remain of their life on the Audrain frontier. Now and then they welcomed into their cabin Colonel Thomas Benton, one of Missouri's first U.S. Senators, passing by on one of his "electioneering tours." In return for their wild turkey, fried venison and warm hospitality, the Senator presented them with a number of public documents, which Young, though he could not read, nailed up on the walls of his cabin. Greatly honored by these official papers and by the Senator's friendship, he named one of his sons after Benton. Unfortunately, while out one day with his mother—"an excellent bee hunter"—looking for honey, the younger Thomas climbed a high grapevine, cut the vine above his head and suffered such a jolting fall that he never quite reached the heights of his famous namesake. For their eldest daughter's wedding the resourceful Mrs. Young baked cakes for their company, grinding their own wheat on a hand mill and sifting the flour through her muslin cap. Mr. Young died in 1833, a victim of his pet bull.

Settlers on the Audrain frontier in general "took to the timber along the streams." Here they could be sure of ample water and a good supply of wood—wood needed for building houses and fences as well as for cooking and warmth. In the county's central portion, where grassland was interspersed with stands of trees and small creek beds, they cleared woods and planted that land first. The prairie remained vacant.

Rarely viewed as a friendly land, the prairie presented problems: scarce drinking water, sod that took three or four teams of oxen and several men to break up for planting, extremes of weather, with violent winds and deep snows, and prairie fires that spread for miles unchecked. Grass grew so thick and tall that a man on horseback could pass unseen by someone only a few yards away. The soil, described as "of a cold, wet, clammy nature," produced little but grass. With few trees to serve as landmarks, people got lost on the open grassland. Farmers felt vulnerable there, clinging instead to the familiar woods. Many dreaded the prairie's loneliness and desolation.

Wild animals, snakes and huge flies also filled their lives with dread. Everyone had to constantly guard against wolves, which were numerous and savage. Even in broad daylight wolves were spotted "skulking" around thickets and "sallying" down paths, "with a sneaking look of mingled cowardice and cruelty." At night, wrote one settler, "the howls of these animals were so loud and incessant that sleep at times was out of the question . . . the whole air seemed to be filled with the vibrations of their most infernal and diabolical music." Rattlesnakes, or "serpents," grew to such an immense size and were found in such numbers and in so many places that they, too, formed a constant source of danger.

The giant green-head flies infesting the prairie caused difficulties of another kind. The "pestiferous Green Head" attacked animals so viciously that oxen, mules, horses and cows could neither work nor graze near the prairie in warm weather. One settler reported seeing horses "bleeding from every pore" after being assailed by the huge flies. The flies decreased only as farmers began to plow up the prairie, leaving, said one, "no resting-place for the soles of the feet of the green-head flies."

By the mid-1830s the whooping of Indians and the howling of wolves had given way to the bleating of sheep, the creaking of wagon wheels and the echoing blows of the farmer's ax. The infernal sounds of the Audrain frontier were steadily yielding to a more civilized song.

4

Salt River Tigers

During their frontier days people in neighboring counties called the Audrain settlers "Salt River Tigers." Although they were good sturdy folk, with a strong and independent spirit, they did show certain cat-like tendencies: a stubborn determination to do things their own way, a firm resolve to be beholden to none, and an almost feline ferocity when crossed. And, of course, they prowled the prairie by night.

Settlers disputed the origin of their nickname. Some connected it to voting. On one occasion a group of Audrain men from around the Salt River grew extremely upset because they could not take part in a current election. Since they were living in unorganized territory this situation was not unexpected but not, they thought, to be tolerated. Determined to vote, they rode over to the nearest Boone County election site, demanding their rights.

A barrel or two of whiskey stood at most polling places in those days, with political supporters ready to supply free drinks for anyone backing their candidate; records do not say whether the Salt River visitors were influenced by this practice. Ready to cast their votes—then done by voice so all could hear—they were refused the privilege and told they were not "legitimate." Loudly protesting this treatment, they persisted so vehemently, and were "so pertinacious, as well as imperative in their demand," that the election judges finally gave in and recorded their votes. Said one ruffled judge, as the intruders left for home, "Ain't those men tigers?"

Another explanation differs. To avoid the dreaded green-head flies that infested the prairie, Audrain settlers traveled in warm weather at night. Setting out around midnight for Paris, Fulton or Louisiana, they arrived before the sun was high and the flies more rabid, and started back home after sundown. To save their livestock from the hordes of flies, they also worked their land after dark, tending their crops by the light of the moon.

All this nocturnal activity made them an object of amusement to outsiders. One farmer wrote that he and his friends were "somewhat the sport of our larger and more powerful neighbors, who would sometimes, good humoredly, call us 'Salt River Tigers.'"

Like the first settlers of mid-Missouri, many of these Audrain pioneers came originally from Virginia, Kentucky and Tennessee. Mostly of British ancestry, many were the self-reliant, high-spirited, independent-minded Scotch-Irish—people well suited to the frontier. As they staked out their land claims, they also staked out their accustomed lifestyle, bringing with them the same methods of farming and building houses, the same attitudes toward politics and slavery, and the same ideas toward religion and education they had known back home. By the mid-1800s this section of Missouri, including Audrain, resembled in many ways the Upper South, its people holding strong emotional ties to their former homes and maintaining strong family bonds with relatives still in the South.

Some settlers immigrated in large groups, bringing with them families, slaves, furniture and household goods; they intended to establish new plantations. Others came as single men, small farmers dependent upon their own labor and eager to make their own way; they often returned east to bring back wives, brothers or friends. Still others came as members of an extended family, joining uncles, married sisters or cousins already settled in the state; they sometimes farmed and sometimes became "mercantile men," opening stores and businesses. Those with relatives already living in Monroe, Boone or Callaway Counties were the first to push into neighboring Audrain.

Among the first to establish farms in the county were Joseph McDonald and "one Wainscot" in 1830, with John Martin close behind. "In the same year," wrote an early historian, "came William Levaugh, John Barnett, Caleb Williams, Black Isam, Fiddler Isam, John Kilgore and Richard Willingham." Soon joining them were families named McIntyre, Pearson, Watts, Byrns, Jackson, Harrison, Haynes, Fenton and "a Mrs. Throgmoten." Within a few years came Faucet, Gant, West, Morris, White, Smith, Mansfield, Powell, Jesse and Blue.

Because living in the wilderness required hard work, the larger the family the better. In the Neil Blue home were ten children; John Barnett had twelve; William Jesse, sixteen, three of whom died young; John B. Morris, thirteen; and John Kilgore, married twice, eighteen—one of whom, Frank, was in 1831 the first child born to settlers in the county. John Bybee, by six wives, was the father of twenty-six.

Life on the frontier was never easy, and Audrain proved no exception. Crude one-room log cabins, built from trees cut down on the site, featured a rough handmade table and a few stools, a primitive bed, a single fireplace and sometimes a greased paper window to let in a little daylight. Clothing, homespun and handmade, was generally sewn from "linsey-woolsey," buckskin or fur. Shoes were often homemade moccasins.

Food centered around coarse bread made from corn or wheat ground by hand; wild game such as duck, turkey or quail; bear or deer meat; chickens and eggs; beans, pumpkins, squash and potatoes; wild grapes and plums; honey, milk and butter—with no sugar and little tea or coffee. Most of what a settler's family had to eat depended on his skill with a rifle and luck with the planting, and his wife's resourceful spirit and talent for cooking. Although they had few of the conveniences common to more civilized areas, in the eyes of many the bounty of the land allowed the settlers to "live well."

In general the frontier favored the strong but sometimes crushed the weak. Illness was frequent and many died young. The various Mrs. Bybees were not alone in passing early to their graves; many a husband outlived more than one wife and several offspring. Not all children survived to adulthood, the pages of countless family Bibles bearing silent witness to numerous births and early deaths.

Most households included grandparents and other relatives, each of whom was expected to contribute to the welfare of the family as a whole. In such isolated conditions all had to care for one another to survive the physical and economic hardships as well as the mental and emotional burdens of pioneer life.

The first settlers of the county, slow to open their wilderness, nevertheless took the first necessary steps, pushing the edge of civilization before them until the frontier around them disappeared. Where once, to and fro by shade of night, Salt River Tigers had prowled the countryside, now they faded into the past as people began to think of themselves as responsible, respectable citizens of the new Audrain County.

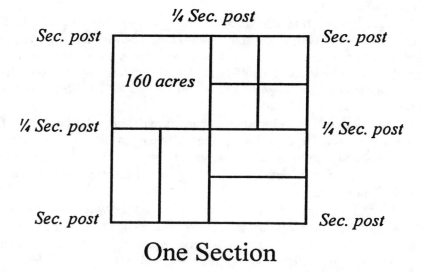

One Section

5

Land, Lots of Land

The United States of America

To all to whom these Presents shall come, Greeting:

Whereas James Harrison . . . has deposited in the General Land Office
. . . a certificate . . . whereby it appears that full payment has been
made by the said James Harrison for . . . Eighty Acres . . . Now Know
Ye that the United States of America . . . have given and granted . . .
unto the said James Harrison and to his heirs, the said tract above
described: to Have and to Hold the same, together with all the rights,
privileges, immunities, and appurtenances of whatsoever nature,
thereunto belonging, unto the said James Harrison and to his heirs
and assigns forever.

By the President—Andrew Jackson

I n this manner did the government of the United States record the sale, at
its Land Office at Palmyra, Missouri, on the fifteenth day of September,
1835, of eighty acres of the public domain to an Audrain settler named
James Harrison. To Harrison, and to every other settler, the land patent he
received—a stiff parchment document bearing the President's seal and sig-
nature—represented the promise of the frontier.

The purchase of land marked a major achievement in a settler's life.
As he carefully placed his patent in a safe place and knelt to sift the soil of
his new land through his fingers, he sensed the opportunity that now lay

before him. As a landowner he made known his intent to settle down, plant crops and become a law-abiding citizen. With land he could make his own way and improve his lot in life, "trusting only to his strong arm and willing heart to work out his ambition for a home for himself and wife, and a competence for his children."

By 1834 there were still not more than thirty families in the entire county. Over the next six years the population slowly increased to nearly two thousand, as others claimed land in this area so long "unmarred by the hand of civilization."

Settlers straggling into Audrain first chose land in the southwest and central areas. With hard cash required for land purchase, they hoarded gold and the family inheritance or borrowed what they could to raise the one hundred dollars needed for the minimum land purchase. Carefully select- ing a desirable site, they then proceeded to make their claim.

Following established policy for the purchase of public lands from the federal government, prospective buyers presented themselves at the nearest U.S. Land Office, where sales were regularly held. Some were en- titled to free "bounty land" as a result of military service in the War of 1812 or the Indian Wars, as much as one hundred acres going to privates and up to five hundred to colonels. Most, however, paid the standard price of $1.25 per acre in hard money (gold, not paper promises), with a required minimum purchase of eighty acres. As soon as they indicated the land of their choice, made payment and were "given the numbers," they recorded their land at the nearest courthouse, usually at Paris or Fulton. Later many claims would be filed again at Mexico.

An essential part of each land transaction was its accurate descrip- tion. Government surveyors marked off land according to a set plan. A principal meridian line running north and south on the map was selected— in Missouri it was the fifth—and parallel range lines were marked at six- mile intervals. These were crossed by lines running east and west, also six miles apart, forming a giant checkerboard of six-mile squares known as congressional townships. Each township was divided into thirty-six pieces called sections. Each section, measuring one mile along each side and num- bered from one to thirty-six, could be divided into halves, quarters and eighths. A full section consisted of 640 acres, a quarter section of 160. A settler buying the minimum eighty acres learned a description such as E/2, SWq, Sec18, T51, R10W to identify his land; once learned, it became as familiar as his wife's name.

Like other settlers filing their claims, on April 23, 1836, at Paris in Monroe County, Robert Mansfield and James Smith filed the plat for their proposed new town of Mexico. Following state law, they also requested the legislature to select it as Audrain's county seat when the county was organized. In order to ensure its selection, they were prepared to give to the new county "every alternate lot and a public square," and to take any other steps required by law. Since there were no other towns in the proposed county, they faced no competition, but did meet some difficulties. They were soon offering an additional tract of land—referred to as the "Donated Addition," west and north of the Original Town—along with the promised lots. Three commissioners, one each from Boone, Callaway and Monroe Counties, were appointed to select the seat of justice and to organize the county.

On December 17, 1836, Missouri officially recognized the county of Audrain, with Mexico named the county seat. For settlers scattered throughout her "trackless wilderness" the hardships of the pioneer experience finally proved worthwhile. They, like so many other Americans, set about improving their land and organizing a government for their county—claiming at last the frontier's full promise.

II

Pioneers, Those Bold and Hardy Men

COUNTIES
CHAPTER XIII.

AUDRAIN COUNTY.

AN ACT, to designate the limits of a county, hereafter to be organized, to be called Audrain county.

Approved January 12, 1831

Sec. 1. *Be it enacted by the General Assembly of the State of Missouri.* That the territory lying and being within their following boundaries, to wit, beginning at the south west corner of the county of Monroe; thence east with the township line, between townships fifty two and fifty three, to where the said township line intersects the western line of Pike county; thence a little east of south with said county line, to the south west corner of Pike county, to where the township line between townships fifty and fifty one, intersects the range line between ranges four and five; thence west with said township line, to where it intersects the rangle line between ranges six and seven, thence south to the North East corner of Callaway county, where the township line between townships forty nine and fifty, intersects the range line between ranges six and seven; thence west, with said township line to where it intersects the Boon (*sic*) county line; thence north with said county line to where it intersects the township line between townships fifty and fifty two; thence west, with said township line to where it intersects the range line between ranges twelve and thirteen; thence north to the beginning, shall be, and the same is hereby designated a contemplated county, to be known by the name of Audrain county:. and so soon as there shall be inhabitants in said territory, sufficient to entitle said designated county to a representative, by the then existing law of the land, the same shall be organized and entitled to all the rights and privileges of other counties in the state.

6

Creating a County

During the early months of 1837 people across America were busy in many ways. In the City of Washington President Andrew Jackson was getting ready to hand the Republic over to President-Elect Martin Van Buren. In Congress Senators Clay, Calhoun and Webster were addressing the state of the Union. In Michigan residents were celebrating statehood; in Texas, remembering the Alamo. In Missouri Governor Lilburn Boggs was battling the Mormons and in Mexico, seat of Audrain, determined settlers were creating a county.

It was not an easy task. Setting up a government in the thinly populated wilderness of Audrain County took patience, fortitude and a good deal of common sense. Much responsibility fell upon county judges and others holding office.

The first meeting of the Audrain County Court, as directed by the governor, was held in Mexico on February 6, 1837. The site was ascribed to the wrong owner, the county seat's name was incorrectly recorded, and one of the county's three judges failed to appear, but the beginning was thought promising. The place where they met—the town's only building, the "business house" of James Fenton and Edward Jennings—stood on the east side of the Square. The first record reads:

> Be it remembered that on Monday the 6th of February, in the year 1837, at the house of Edward Jennings, in the county of Audrain and town of New Mexico, James Harrison and James E. Fenton, Esq.,

produced their commissions from his Excellency, the Governor of the State of Missouri, appointing them county justices in and for the said county of Audrain, which together with the certificate of their qualifications, was duly read. Whereupon, proclamations being made by William Levaugh, elisor, court was duly opened and proceeded to business.

After the commissions for Harrison and Fenton were read, Joel Haynes was sworn in as clerk. The appointed sheriff, James Jackson, declined to serve and refused to change his mind, leaving that office temporarily vacant. With this fact noted, court adjourned.

The Court met again the next day, with Hezekiah I. M. Doan, the third commissioner, present and James Harrison, the first presiding judge, conducting the meeting. The first item of business granted a liquor license to one of the judges:

> On the motion of James E. Fenton, leave is granted him for selling and retailing spirituous liquors and groceries at his house in the town of New Mexico, in this county, for six months from the 17th day of December, 1836, upon his paying a tax of $5; also a tax of one-eighth per cent on every $150.

The Court's second order set up the county's five townships: Saling, Wilson, Salt River, Prairie and Loutre. With each directed to name two constables and two justices of the peace, elections were ordered at designated houses. The third item on that day's agenda, the granting of a second liquor license in Mexico—this one to George Turley—completed the business of the first session.

The Court convened for its second session a month later on March 20, 1837, making several appointments: Ackley Day, commissioner for the sale of public lots, Joseph Pearson, justice of the peace for the Salt River Township and, at an annual salary of $14.00, John A. Henderson, county treasurer.

It was then decided that as soon as possible a temporary courthouse should be built on lot 6, block 8, on the south side of the Square. George Turley and James Fenton were named supervisors and directed to build a one-story, two-room house of "good white oak hewed logs" and "a good roof of shingles."

The Court turned next to road petitions. Roads were of great importance since anyone crossing the prairie, guided only by "course or direction," was "likely to wander at random and be lost." The first proposed a road to "commence at the west end of Love street . . . and extend westwardly to intersect the road leading from Columbia . . . crossing the South fork of Salt River, between Ackley Day's and Thomas Hooks', and up the prairie between the South fork and Skull lick." This was approved and three commissioners appointed to "view the road."

The commissioners were instructed to widen current paths by clearing more trees and to blaze and notch trees along the trails to indicate a "public highway." They were also to plow furrows across the prairie to establish more direct routes to specified places. These early roads usually went "as the crow flies"; later courts would pay more attention to section lines. Before adjourning the Court approved a second road east to Danville and a third from the Square to Fulton.

With the framework for governing in place, officials proceeded with their assigned duties. The first deed recorded was dated February 5, 1837. William Wood of Audrain sold forty acres of land described as the ne1/4, SW1/4, Sec36, T51, R9, to John B. Morris of Audrain for the sum of $102.50 "in hand paid to the said William Wood."

The county's first marriage certificate, issued by the clerk and placed in the records, read:

> Be it remembered that I, Robert A. Younger, one of the ministers of the M.E. Church, did on the 2d day of February, 1837, solemnize the rites of matrimony, between Samuel Riggs and Nancy Dollins, of Audrain county, and joined them together as man and wife.

Other early licenses went to Jesse Robards and Barthena Smith on June 22, 1837; Joseph A. Peery and Harriet Talley, September 19, 1837; John Pearson and Mary Barson, December 21, 1837; and on February 8, 1838, by the Reverend Robert Mansfield, Lycurgus L. Ramsay and Jane Fenton. Years later the latter bride would be remembered as "intelligent and accomplished," with a wedding dress "made of elegant white flowered satin, being unadorned except by the charms of the beautiful wearer . . . magnificent!"

Collecting taxes proved to be a major undertaking for the first officials. Since there was little cash in backwoods areas and because they were trying to eliminate wolves, the State of Missouri allowed taxes to be paid with wolf scalps. Some "hard cash," or gold, was collected, but wolf scalps made up a large portion of the county's early revenue.

Although accounts vary, the amount of taxes collected by the county during its first year appears to have been $45.92. Revenue due the state for the next year, 1838, came to around $112.91—$40 in hard money and the rest in wolf scalps.

Taxes were low; men "in good circumstances" paid from 37 and 1/2 cents to 50 cents per year. Morris, the county's wealthiest resident, in 1840 paid $5.11 on his farm outside of Mexico. For years taxes reflected the county's small population, the total locally for 1839 being $165.67, and for 1840, $234.20.

Jack Willingham, sheriff and collector, was responsible for delivering tax money to Jefferson City. Some say he rode horseback, others that he walked. On one trip he wound up lending a friend the entire amount of public money in his possession. As one settler remembered it:

> On his way to Jefferson City, Jack met Uncle Charley McIntyre going to a neighbor to buy some nice cattle he had selected, and Uncle Charley, wishing to get them on the best terms possible, desired to pay cash. He learned of Jack that he was taking the money to the capital, and immediately entered into a negotiation for a loan. Jack turned the money over to Uncle Charley and then returned home, and in due course of time, Uncle Charley returned the revenue to Jack, and thus Uncle Charley was accommodated; the State lost nothing, and Audrain county came up nobly to her credit, and the sheriff never defaulted.

Though limited at times in experience and ability, early county officials were, with one notable exception, honest and upright citizens. With his partner, Jennings, having departed the area by 1838, County Judge Fenton was himself gone by 1850. He had supplied building materials for the new courthouse under questionable circumstances and had performed other official "duties" considered improper by some, reflecting, wrote an early historian, the "loose methods of doing business in those days."

Most early officeholders, however, were regarded as capable public servants who held to a standard of conduct greatly benefiting the county. Their casual approach to governing and slow progress in getting things done, typical of the time and place, were tempered by a sense of "individual responsibility, individual duty and individual moral manhood."

All Audrain settlers contributed to its growth and development. Perhaps none did more than the small group of men who created the county and set it on its course.

7

Justice Askew

The quality of justice in early Audrain County, while not strained, might be described as slightly askew. It was not absent; within three months of the county's organization a circuit judge was holding court. It was not ignored; residents regarded with respect the presence of law and order. Nor was it partial. Common sense and expediency simply overpowered, at times, the pursuit of justice.

During its first few years life in the county was crude and unsophisticated and the conduct of many of its residents deemed "rude and uncivilized." This conduct often centered around drinking, betting and "gaming at cards." Grand juries called to eliminate such illegal activities usually refused to bring charges, since the jurors themselves frequently practiced the same behavior. Poker players constantly being brought into court were rarely found guilty because most juries included their gambling companions. In one case the defense attorney argued the merits of card-playing, winning a verdict of not guilty for his client by proving to judge and jury that "poker was a game of science and not of chance."

Along with gambling, liquor consumption flourished. Mexico's two dram shops and other sources of distilled spirits supplied many with "intoxicants" not only for leisure hours but also for the working day. Those relishing their liquor, referred to as "rollickers," frequented the Square and public events, replenishing their supply at Fenton's store or Turley's tavern and sometimes rollicking into the night.

Election campaigns provided opportunities for many to indulge, the combination of "inflammatory speeches" and free liquor proving irresistible to Whigs and Democrats alike. The county's first presidential campaign took place in 1840 with William Henry Harrison running against Martin Van Buren. Heralded by chants of *Tippecanoe and Tyler, Too* and promising *$2 per day and roast beef,* it aroused even backwoods areas such as Audrain into political frenzy much enhanced by "potations of hard cider." On election day barrels of whiskey stood near the Court House door and in the yards of most voting houses across the county. Backers for each party poured free drinks for all, urged support for their candidates and sometimes rewarded a "correct" vote with an extra drink.

With elections neither written nor secret, a man called his vote aloud—and sometimes had to defend his choice. Arguments arising over a candidate's political beliefs often flared into fights. Fights broke out also after ballots were counted, particularly if results did not match an expected outcome. As much a part of an election day as the voting itself were the drinking and fighting.

Other opportunities abounded for betting, brawling and imbibing. Saturday afternoons saw horse races at the town track, a dusty matted-down stretch of grass and mud running a rough half-mile from Jefferson Street east along Promenade. Races prompted fervent interest and wild betting, winners raking in produce, hard money, items of clothing, horses—"anything from a quart of whiskey to a town lot."

Fistfights threatened to erupt anywhere, anytime. Card games, wrestling matches, foot races and shooting matches produced rivalries that waxed fierce. Spectators and participants stood ready to bet on any activity as well as on the expected "fisticuffs." Some may have argued that a few wagers and minor altercations relieved the boredom of the town's routine; they certainly promoted the disturbance of the town's peace.

Officials faced difficulties in keeping that peace. Charged with the maintenance of law and order, the sheriff could select deputies to serve for specific purposes, but each depended primarily upon the cooperation of the public. Audrain, unlike other counties, for several years had no jail; any wrongdoer had to be personally guarded at the Court House. A minor lawbreaker, promising to appear in court, might be allowed to remain at home. Serious offenders, of which there were few, were escorted to the Monroe County jail.

No lawyers then lived in the county—the first would not arrive until the early 1850s. Except for the county-circuit clerk, the legal apparatus for any circuit court proceeding had to be brought into town along with the circuit judge. Early court sessions took place in Fenton's store, with jurors retiring to the hazel bushes at the corner of Jefferson and Jackson Streets to reach a verdict. In one such proceeding the defense attorney strolled by, continued his argument to the jury, and won his client an acquittal.

The Audrain County Circuit Court, assigned to Missouri's Fourth Judicial Circuit, Judge Priestly H. McBride presiding, began its first term on March 13, 1837. The judge's appointment and that of the circuit attorney, John Heard, were duly noted. The next day the commission's report on the county seat was "received, examined and approved" by Judge McBride, who then opened court.

The first case before him was that of the state against Richard Bryant, "upon indictment for larceny." The second was against Samuel Mounts, also for stealing. These were tried at later sessions, the Mounts case being dismissed and a verdict of not guilty brought for Bryant. Other early cases included *The State of Missouri v Samuel Turner, Betting on Poker* and *The State of Missouri v Vincent Moore, Betting at Three Up.*

At its second session, in July 1837, the court opened at Fenton's store but soon moved to the temporary courthouse. Several lawyers from nearby counties were enrolled at this session. Jurors included, among others, George Cardwell, H. I. M. Doan, Isham C. Kilgore, Robert C. Mansfield, Benjamin B. Wilkerson and George Turley. Around a half-dozen cases were heard, with court lasting two days.

In accord with state law, circuit court met four times a year. By the quarterly session of November 1838, it had on its docket nineteen civil cases, mostly involving debt, eight indictments for assault and battery, seven cases for playing poker and two for keeping gaming houses. It would be ten years before a divorce suit appeared: on April 29, 1847, Elizabeth Gass was granted a divorce from David Gass.

The first murder trial in the county was that of the State of Missouri against Milroy Powell "for killing George Eubanks with a hoe." The incident took place on a farm near Mexico on July 6, 1840, causing an uproar in the community. With the defendant pleading self-defense, the jury returned a verdict of manslaughter in the fourth degree. Powell was fined $325, taken to Monroe County for imprisonment—and released before his sentence expired.

In another murder case the accused was said to have vanished into the night. After an evening of drinking and playing cards at a local tavern, James Hall and Samuel Dingle had greeted the morning with "a spirited altercation of words" that led to a furious fight with chairs. Hall then "drew his dirk" and "struck Dingle several blows." Dingle staggered out on the porch, slumped against a post, "fell forward on his face and expired." Bound over to the circuit court, Hall was granted a change of venue to Boone County. The sheriff and several guards set out with him to Columbia, stopped for the night at a small farmhouse on the way, and explained later that they were eating supper, the door was open, the night was "very dark" and the prisoner simply disappeared. And was never seen again.

Despite such "hilarious doings," as one observer described them, the county finally succeeded in establishing law and order. Within a few years residents recognized more signs of responsible government and stable society. On the Square stood the Court House. Churches organized. The racetrack "removed to a respectable distance." Rollickers either left town or reformed. Volatile emotions calmed down.

Justice prevailed. Justice properly administered, prudently restrained, uniformly balanced and, at last, carefully set aright.

8

The Taming of the Square

$\mathbb{W}$hen the county of Audrain was organized the tiny village of Mexico consisted of little more than four dusty lanes marking off the "Publick Square," a few "rude log dwellings" scattered here and there amidst the brush, and a population described as "only a handful." Despite the founders' glowing hopes, progress proved slow. After its first few buildings went up it would be a decade and more before the little town could claim much growth.

During the early months of 1836 and into the fall, James Smith and Robert Mansfield were busy platting the county's prospective seat of justice. Familiar with problems caused by towns that sprang up haphazardly, only later to be chosen as county seats, state officials had recently directed that new county seats be set up according to an orderly plan, with space designated for public buildings. For Mexico the founders used the Shelbyville Square Plan that guided many Missouri county seats after the 1820s.

The initial plat of Mexico consisted of one large grid marked off into twenty-five blocks known as the Original Town. Each block, measuring 240 feet square, was divided into eight lots and intersected by a 12-foot alley; between the blocks ran streets 60 feet wide. In choosing names for the four main business streets around the central square, the founders reflected the typical settler's strong democratic leanings; no Adams or Madison was so honored, but rather Washington, Jefferson, Monroe and the current president, Andrew Jackson.

The first sale of lots donated by the founders to the county, amounting to half the town, took place May 4, 1837, with a second sale the following November. Under the supervision of Ackley Day, appointed by the county court, the auction was open to all. It was the sale of these town lots that soon began to fill the county treasury.

Heading the list for the first sale was the name of Eli Smith, who bought lots 1 and 8 in block 1 for $5 each. Next, lots 1 and 8 in block 2 went to Joel Haynes for a total of $18.50. With prices varying according to location, block 3 was desirable, as were lots in blocks 4, 13 and 17. The highest sale amounted to $63.50 for lot 4, block 17. The next highest amount came from William S. Williams, who paid $60 for lot 8, block 13. All of block 5 went for $38.50. George Turley bought the lot at the northeast corner of the Square. James Fenton bought lot 4 in block 3 for $30, plus four others.

Several locations were reserved, at least on paper, for specific purposes. Block 25, in the middle of the Original Town, was designated for the Court House and Public Square. Reserved for a seminary, which never came to be, were lots 6 and 7 in block 6. A market proposed for lot 2, block 16, was never built, nor was a schoolhouse intended for lot 8, block 21. In the Donated Addition, that extra area the founders gave the county, a block in the far northwest corner was reserved for the village cemetery—and would soon be used, the first grave being that of William Cardwell.

Even before its official designation as county seat, some Mexico lots had been sold. One—lot 6, block 12—on the Square's east side, had gone to James Fenton, whose crude "business house" saw the county's first official proceedings. Several lots north of the Square went to John B. Morris.

Morris had made it known that once the county seat was assured he would build a large house on lot 4 of block 21, north of Love Street and east of Jefferson, that would serve as a tavern, a general merchandise store and a home for his family. As the first "improvement" in town since Fenton's, it attracted much attention across the county. Representing a major financial commitment by a respected businessman, the venture provided an incentive for other merchants and residents, established an important trading place, and promoted stability for the town. It also promised to everyone in the Audrain wilds good food and decent lodging.

During the summer of 1837 the county court moved into the temporary courthouse and by the fall of 1838, with the county coffers sufficiently full, was making plans for the permanent courthouse. Following directions from the legislature, three commissioners were named who were to decide upon a plan for the building, place announcements in public places and award the contract "by crying and knocking off the same to the loest bidder."

The new Court House cost $1,600. Unpretentious in design, the square, "old style" brick structure of two stories with a hip roof proved to be a satisfactory public building in keeping with Audrain's status as a new rural county. On the first floor was a large bare courtroom and on the second, three smaller rooms. The front entrance faced east on Jefferson. Although some counties first built a jail, it would be several years before Audrain's jail went up, across Washington on the Square's west side.

The largest and most substantial building in the village, the Court House dominated not only the Square but the little town itself. Completed in the fall of 1839, for thirty years it would serve the county. Within its walls deeds were recorded, wills probated and licenses issued; circuit court met four times a year. Religious services and political meetings were held in its courtroom, news of importance announced from its front steps and countywide barbecues enjoyed in its yard.

Such a barbecue was held on Independence Day, July 4, 1848. It was a "clear pleasant day," reported one observer, with "upwards of six hundred in attendance." The Reverend Mansfield began the program by reading the Declaration of Independence. County Judge Jim Jackson, running for reelection, spoke for fifteen minutes and Dr. L. N. Hunter "made an oration, which of course was good." The barbecue, also pronounced "good," was followed by dancing, with all activity ended by sunset. Despite the large crowd, "all passed off quietly and in order."

By the late 1840s Mexico consisted of the Fenton House on the Square's east side; the temporary courthouse, now a store, on the south; and on the west, off Washington and down in a hollow, Charles Ward's blacksmith shop. At its northeast corner George Turley sold groceries and intoxicants, and at the southwest corner James Fenton ran a tavern.

South of the Square, west of Jefferson Street on Promenade, sat the small new Methodist Church; when it was built the racetrack moved farther out, eventually ceasing its operation. To the west, near the corner of Jackson and Water Street—later to be called Clark—was located a large pond; ten feet deep in places, it provided drinking water for the town and swimming for youngsters. On Washington, a block north of the Square, sat a small frame meetinghouse that served as church and school. Over to the east, on Jefferson, Mansfield and Smith ran a general store opposite the Morris House, and somewhere nearby was located another tavern referred to as "the Prairie House."

Life in the little village moved as slowly as the cows that ambled into the Square on summer mornings to escape the prairie's heat and flies. Horses, cows, sheep and "old man Bomar's jennets" grazed in the Court House yard, often blocking the path to the door. Depending on the season, pigs rooted in the mud or dust of North Jefferson Street. Dogs roamed at random and chickens scratched near every outside door. At noonday people wandered back and forth around the Square; at sundown silence fell thick and deep across the town.

Every week or so the mail carrier brought news of the outside world and delivered a few letters. On most Sundays a traveling preacher held church service, sometimes performing a marriage. Occasionally, if he had business there, a man would ride horseback up to Paris or down to Fulton, but rarely much farther. Wives gathered when they could for quilting bees, young people for candy pullings and courting couples for moonlight watermelon feasts "on the prairie."

People went about their daily lives, doing the chores, minding the children, tending to business—and bringing society's order to the little town of Mexico.

9

The Green Tree Tavern

J udge John Bingle Morris was regarded by most early residents as Audrain's outstanding pioneer settler and Mexico's foremost founding father. A landholder in the county before its organization, Morris built the first "improvement" in Mexico after its designation as county seat, operated a successful store, served as the town's first postmaster, held the offices of county clerk and county judge for many years and, in a unique contribution to the early settlers, operated the Green Tree Tavern.

He was born in Pendleton County, Kentucky, in 1806. In 1827 he married a neighbor's daughter, the sixteen-year-old Julia Ann Shumate— "of the old Virginia family of that name"—and within three years immigrated to Missouri. Temporarily settling in Callaway County, by 1836 he had bought land in Audrain and was planning to open a "merchandising business" and tavern in Mexico.

By June of 1837 he was hiring workers to build, in the block north of Love Street and east of Jefferson, the large business house that would long be known as the Morris House or Green Tree Tavern. Once begun, it did not take long to finish. George Bomar was named chief contractor; working with him were John Willingham, John Jesse, Reverend Mansfield and Dicky Watts, who every day walked nine miles to the job and nine miles back home.

Each man supplied his own tools for the project, Bomar in particular having at the time a valued red-handled axe. As head contractor he was paid 50 cents a day, the usual workday being from sunup to sundown. The others earned "three bits," or 37 and 1/2 cents a day, with everyone present qualifying also for "three big drinks of whiskey." After some discussion, Jesse and Bomar decided to give Watts, who did the heavy cutting and hewing, two of their own daily draughts of whiskey; Watts could then claim as many as seven drinks a day, an amount thought sufficient to keep him on the job and happy.

Logs were cut in the Brushy Branch area southeast of town, loaded on a "stoneboat," and hauled to the site by oxen—helping with this were two of Willingham's slaves. The finished building was described as a large house with puncheon floors, two fireplaces, seven rooms and one great-room. The addition of wooden benches along the walls of the great-room offered a finishing touch thought nice for the interior of an inn. A welcome addition to Mexico, the Green Tree Tavern proved an immediate asset to its owner.

At some point in the summer of 1837 Morris opened his new enterprise and moved his family, traveling by ox-cart, from Callaway up to Mexico. In addition to several slaves brought with them from Kentucky, the family now consisted of four children. There would eventually be thirteen, all of whom lived to adulthood: Mary, George, Joseph, Isabelle, Peyton, Thomas, Albert, Charles, Eliza, Lucy, Alice, John and William. Peyton, born shortly after their arrival in Mexico, was the first child born in the new village. To better accommodate his growing family Morris soon built a second house, leaving the larger to serve as the store and tavern.

The Green Tree Tavern before long became renowned across the wilderness of northeast Missouri for its hospitality. A variety of visitors frequented the inn: politicians out on a campaign, lawyers coming to circuit court sessions, mercantile men up from St. Louis or St. Charles and travelers finding their way into Mexico. While many guests stayed only one night, a few made the tavern their home, boarding for weeks at the time, and others took midday meals there.

Always glad to welcome a visitor, Morris spread a good table, with an abundance of food. One house specialty was hoecakes; another favorite was ham—one winter he paid a dollar for a hundred bushels of hickory nuts to feed his hogs. Recalled a frequent guest, "No house in the State surpassed it in the deliciousness of its culinary department."

Besides managing his hospitable tavern, Morris also operated a general store. Most of his stock was sent by boat from St. Charles up the Missouri to Portland in Callaway County, and then hauled by oxen and wagon up to Mexico. Goods also came down by land from Hannibal and Louisiana.

In a day when people raised their own chickens and vegetables, hunted their own meat, kept their own cows and ground their own flour, customers at the Morris store shopped mainly for such staples as tea, green coffee, maple sugar and New Orleans molasses. Prices reflected the frontier surroundings; generally corn sold for 5 to 10 cents a bushel, wheat for 30 cents a bushel and bacon for 1 and 1/2 cents a pound. Eggs cost 3 to 5 cents per dozen, honey and butter 5 cents a pound and frying chickens 2 dollars per dozen.

Women, responsible for clothing their families, bought hand cards for wool, cotton and linsey goods, spinning wheels, sewing supplies and leather. Men found such necessities as rifles, axes, bars of lead, gunpowder and "black navy tobacco." Quinine, used to treat "the ague," was no doubt also available. Many customers, having little cash, purchased goods with animal pelts, the most desirable being beaver, otter, raccoon and mink, which Morris traded with dealers in St. Charles.

The Morris Tavern also served as Mexico's first post office, with Morris commissioned the first postmaster in 1837. By 1838, when the county held its first local election, he was also standing for county-circuit clerk, an office he easily won. After that position was divided he remained as county clerk, serving until 1858. He was then elected county judge, a position he held with some interruption through the Civil War years. After the war he won three more elections to the court, at his death being its presiding judge.

Over his many years in the county, through his various positions, he consistently provided honest, firm leadership. He "adhered tenaciously," said one settler, "to whatever he thought to be right." When he died in 1875 at the age of 67, he was remembered as a public servant of "sterling character and great firmness." The Audrain County Bar passed a resolution commending him for his many contributions, calling him a man "of large public spirit and enterprise" who had long "labored for the development, prosperity and happiness of his county and fellow-citizens."

But he is remembered best for the tavern that for many years graced the tiny village. With his ready hospitality Morris, perhaps more than anyone, fostered among the people of Audrain the customs and manners of their common Virginia and Kentucky heritage. Over those early years settlers gathered at his inn for many activities: large meals to which everyone came for some special celebration, political rallies that began or ended with suitable refreshment, quilting bees, candy-pullings and barbecues. Dances, though frowned upon by some as "sinful," highlighted many a holiday. As many as a hundred men and women sometimes crowded the tavern, "treading the maze of dance" to such favorites as "Chicken Pie" and "Buffalo Gals"—tunes that "permeated their very souls."

In later years settlers recalled with affection the Green Tree Tavern, always mentioning it as central to the town's pioneer days. They remembered well its open door of friendship, dinners of ham and buttermilk and, "irresistibly happyfying in its effects," fiddlers sounding the notes for a Virginia Reel.

10

Learning Their Letters

Early Audrain settlers had little time for reading, writing or ciphering. Food, shelter and a livelihood demanded their complete attention. As more families moved into the county, however, education became more important. Some were soon insisting that their children "learn their letters."

Many early settlers had themselves been given no chance for schooling. Unable to read, they were often suspicious of education. A man was valued more for his physical prowess—the better to chop down a tree and build a cabin—than for any "book-learning." Others had been well educated and were eager to instill in their children a respect for formal knowledge. They led the way in forming schools and promoting in the new county a high regard for education.

The earliest attempts at providing schools came from parents joining with neighbors to pay a young man or woman to teach in their homes; later, schoolhouses were built. Parents subscribed, or paid a fee, for each child attending such a subscription school, the combined fees making up the teacher's salary. The teacher, often a relative or neighbor, had usually received some basic schooling, though little more, and was willing to teach the rudiments of learning to children obviously in need of them.

The county's first schools functioned without public funds, lasted for indefinite periods of time and varied as to the quality of education. For a short time in the early 1830s a teacher named John Cassidy conducted a small school in the southern part of the county. Other early schools were Union, in the same area, and Beagles, northeast of Mexico.

Union School, regarded by many as the county's first subscription school, opened in 1832. Located at the northeast corner of Section 35, Township 50, Range 9, it was organized by Matthew Scott, Temple Wayne, Thom- as Boyd, Mrs. Jane Gregg, Lewis and Ackley Day. Making the best of materials at hand, they built a one-room log schoolhouse with a dirt floor, furnishing it with a few rough benches. Archibald Gregg served as the first teacher of the dozen or so children belonging to these families.

Mexico parents took similar steps toward providing an education for their children, a Mrs. Penny being one early teacher. Another, beginning his school in 1843, was John P. Clark. Self-educated but well read, he soon gained a "wide and enviable reputation as a teacher." Within a few years he had given up teaching for real estate and to serve as circuit clerk, leaving Mexico again without a school.

Miss Susan Van Arsdale was then invited to open a school in town. Young, capable and popular she had held sessions for several county families. "I expect to teach school in Mexico this coming summer," she noted in her diary that spring, a few weeks later adding, "Commenced school in Mexico May 1st, 1848. 26 scholars the first week." Larger than her previous groups, this school met in the meetinghouse on the west side of Washington Street, a block north of the Square. Varying from week to week according to how many parents paid their fees, its enrollment at one point reached thirty-eight, age five to late teens, and lasted into September with no additional session promised. "Closed my school of 5 months," reads another entry. "It averaged twenty-five scholars and amounted to almost 90 dollars."

Education in these schools corresponded to the first three years of primary instruction. Emphasis was placed on the ABCs, writing, reading and "oral and mental arithmetic." Pupils memorized spelling words and arithmetic tables, saying them aloud in unison, and spent much time copying information from the blackboard or the teacher's book into their own copybooks. Every pupil was expected to at least learn to read, write his name and recite his numbers to the rule of three. Some advanced much further, the level of achievement as a rule being more the result of individual aptitude and desire than high expectations by parents or teacher.

A pupil's school supplies consisted of a goose quill pen, a home-made copybook of brown paper and a small bottle of ink concocted of boiled sumac or pokeberries with a few drops of whiskey added to keep it from freezing. With no textbooks, a teacher usually relied upon a crude blackboard, a Webster's *Blueback Speller,* perhaps a prized reader and one or two Bibles brought from home.

In the school's one room were boys and girls of all ages and learning levels. Discipline posed problems, but parents always backed the teacher. If a child got a tongue-lashing or a whipping at school he could expect another at home; most dared not misbehave.

Attendance, haphazard at best, depended upon the weather, activities at home or in town and the prevalence among pupils and teacher alike of any illness, particularly "the ague." A set schedule was difficult to maintain, the daily routine frequently being interrupted. One teacher once took his gun into the woods at noon recess and returned with a dead wildcat—"a great curiosity to the pupils."

Parents were not alone in their concern for education. Both state and national governments considered it of great importance. The first land ordinances passed by Congress provided that section 16 of each township— or funds from its sale—be reserved for education. Missouri's constitution stated that in each township a school should be set up "as soon as practicable and necessary, where the poor would be taught gratis." Officials, however, were slow in setting up a public school system. The county received its first state funds in 1845, $98.78 to be distributed among schools in four townships, including Union and Beagles. Its 1846 allotment came to $133.40 with little increase or further organization until after the Civil War.

During the 1850s Mexico parents made several efforts to set up "high schools," but none lasted long. In 1852 lots at the southwest corner of Coal and Promenade Streets were sold to the "trustees of a school to be known as the Prairie high school," but no further record remains of the school.

A few years later, in 1855, Professor William Hurt of Columbia's Christian College organized the Prairie Institute, where "every branch of a truly American education will be taught to young ladies and gentlemen." M. Y. Duncan, a young man from Columbia, was hired for the five-month term, with students paying tuition of $8 to $12 for "regular courses," plus Latin and Greek. But this, too, was short-lived.

In 1858 eight "public-spirited men of the community," including former teachers Clark and Duncan, established the Audrain Christian Seminary under the sponsorship of the local Christian Church. With donations amounting to five thousand dollars they built a two-story white frame building of eight rooms on property near the end of South Jefferson Street. Open to boys as well as girls, this school educated some of Mexico's finest until the Civil War forced it to close.

During the war formal education throughout the county came to a standstill. Once again the pursuit of education gave way to practical reality. Only after the return of peace could Audrain children turn again to learning their letters.

Our Flourishing and Proud County

11

Smitten with Gold Fever

$\mathbb{T}$ he cry of "Gold!" that echoed across the valleys of California in 1848 carried swiftly eastward to St. Louis, New York and the rest of the world—and steadily inland to small sleepy villages, rough frontier farmsteads and backwoods Audrain County. The excitement accompanying the news had the "character of a mania" and was compared to a raging fever. Some in the county fell victim, joining thousands of other Americans in heading west to seek gold.

Amazing reports flowed out of California, mesmerizing everyone with glowing accounts of riches to be had for the digging. By late fall of 1848 instead of subsiding, the fever was "rising higher and higher." During that winter, wrote an early Audrain historian, "the one great subject of discussion around the firesides" was gold.

It was said that at one time "the majority of the able-bodied men of the county" were "unsettled in mind," and "contemplating the trip to California." Reflecting in part the difficulty and monotony of their lives, by spring, 116 of the county's 3,200 residents remained steadfast in their resolve. "Smitten with the contagion," they organized a company called the Gold Placers of California.

Joining the Audrain Gold Placers were some of the county's earliest residents, newcomers recently settled, bachelors with no family, men with wives and children, "men with gray beards" and "boys still in their teens." Captain Levi Blount would lead the company, which was typical of many across the nation. The names of Alfred Powell, G. W. Cardwell, John G.

Muldrow, Dr. Nathaniel Allison, Rufus S. Pearson, Alfred Cauthorn, Joseph D. Morris and James B. Kilgore, among others, were listed on the roster, along with several Throckmortons and Cobbses, Isaac, a free man, and "Dan Tucker, a negro."

Three women were named as accompanying their husbands on the long trek: Mrs. Grizelda Powell Blount, the captain's wife, who with their one child at the last minute did not go; Mrs. J. Ridgeway and two children; and Mrs. Jane Humphreys, who was to die along the way. Despite dangers and the possibility of never returning home, all seemed ready and eager to seek the "glittering and precious ore" that lay among the hills beside the Pacific.

They were encouraged by the steady stream of emigrants traveling through Missouri, forming "sights that may never be seen again in Audrain county." One local observer wrote that there was "one continuous line of wagons from the Orient to the Occident, as far as the eye could reach, moving steadily westward." Cows pulled some of the wagons, while some of the prospective gold diggers hauled their worldly goods in handcarts. Oblivious to the practical aspects of such a journey, they fixed their eyes on the western sun and their hearts on the glories of gold.

Three routes lay open to "forty-niners" seeking gold. The water route took them down the coast of South America by ship, around Cape Horn and up the coast to California. The second route deposited the emigrant by ship in Panama, which he crossed on foot or horseback through the jungle to the west coast, from there to sail north. The third route, and the only one feasible for the Audrain Placers, was the overland route: west to Independence, over the Oregon Trail, across the Rockies and along the California Bypass into the promised paradise. Though "sadder farewells were never spoken," on an early spring day in 1849 the "gold-hunters of Audrain" left their homes, slipped into a wagon train and headed west—"Off to Californy," as the popular song went, "my wash-pan on my knee."

Wagon trains faced a multitude of dangers ranging from hostile Indians to violent weather, wild animals and dread disease. Mexico's Dr. Allison was selected "to guard the health" of the group, particularly from the cholera that everyone feared—and that would devastate many a similar group of forty-niners. Convinced that the disease was caused by filth, he insisted that lime be sprinkled at each campsite and that all drinking water be boiled. Except for the unfortunate Mrs. Humphreys, whose fate was not clarified, no one in the group died, a remarkable record for such an undertaking.

The Audrain Gold Placers left no official record of their time in California. A few remained in the West. Most returned to Missouri with enough gold to start a business or build a house, but none with a vast fortune.

Dr. Allison, as he had promised his wife, returned in 1850. Taking the Panama route home, he proceeded up the Mississippi by steamer, where his concern for cholera again proved valuable, for at his insistence the decks were swabbed with lime and a suspected outbreak stopped. Providing medical care in exchange for gold, during his travels he accumulated a substantial supply of gold bars. Unfortunately, many of them were inside his South Jefferson Street home when a few years later it was burglarized and burned to the ground.

On that same voyage home there was on board at least one more Audrain Countian (and probably others), Alfred Cauthorn. He was credited with maintaining the morale of the Gold Placers, being held in high esteem "even by the most wicked of the company." Every evening on the long trip out he gathered his companions around the campfire for devotions. It was said that he was the only man to take his religion to California and return with it untarnished. On the sea leg of the journey home, when a fierce storm threatened the ship, Dr. Allison found him in his cabin, calmly singing the familiar hymn "How Firm a Foundation." At least one fellow passenger then crept to his side and during the remainder of the storm, "sat in comparative composure."

Most of the Audrain gold seekers regarded their journey not in terms of riches acquired, but hardships overcome, spectacular sights seen and status gained from being a part of the Gold Rush. In winters to come, around their own firesides, they often recalled the excitement of going west and the thrill of seeking gold.

One of the Audrain boys, Christopher Columbus Cassidy, on the eve of their departure in 1849, wrote a farewell poem that caught the spirit of the group's great adventure. Among its lines:

Farewell, farewell, my native land, I leave thee only with a sigh,
To wander o'er a foreign strand, Perchance to live, perhaps to die . . .
O'er the broad plains far away, Beyond the Rocky Mountain's crest,
Our wayward feet awhile shall stray, And press the gold besprinkled
west . . .

And in the lapse of coming years, Should fortune be not too unkind,
We'll hope reward for parting tears, In smiles from those we left behind.
We go—yet hoping to return, Friends of our youth, to home and you,
For these do cause our hearts to yearn, E'en when we sigh Adieu—
Adieu.

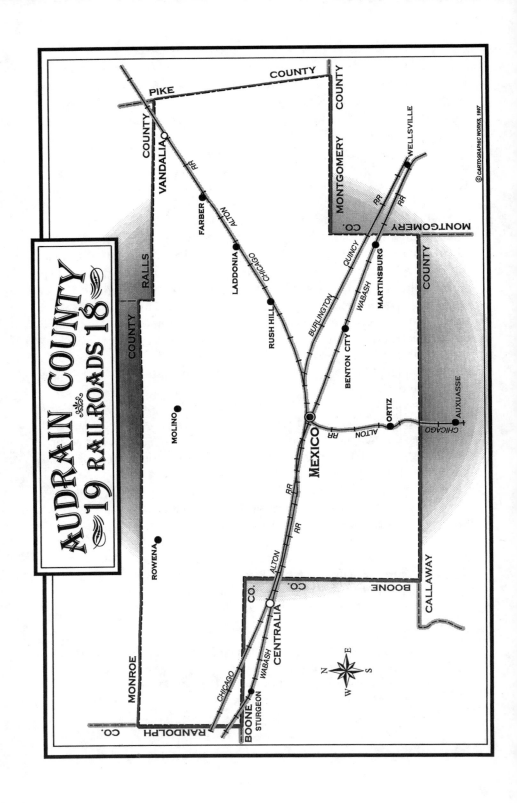

AUDRAIN COUNTY
19 RAILROADS 18

12

All Aboard for Mexico!

I t wasn't the Wabash Cannonball that came streaking into town on that bright spring day in 1858. It was Old Ajax. Old Ajax, chugging down the track, puffing steam, sounding its whistle—and opening for Mexico and Audrain County a direct route, via the railroad, to progress and prosperity.

The first steam engine to enter Mexico, Old Ajax had just ridden the line west from "Jefftown" (Martinsburg) and "Wellsburg"—the newest section of the North Missouri Railroad. One of the earliest in the state, the North Missouri Railroad Company, chartered in 1851, was constructing a freight and passenger line from St. Louis northwest toward Iowa, along the high land between the Missouri and Mississippi Rivers. By following this "ridge route," the line cut straight across Audrain County, promising untold benefits.

Founded in the midst of a "trackless prairie," Mexico for its first two decades had never been able to generate much commerce. Early settlers with great difficulty hauled a few crops by wagon and drove their hogs and cattle overland to the nearest markets at Hannibal, Louisiana or St. Charles. By the 1840s and 1850s the Dingle brothers' teamster operation was carrying crops and supplies for farmers and merchants to and from market by oxen and wagon; a strenuous undertaking, it allowed Mexico stores to stock only a few goods for local customers.

With a railroad, however, town leaders anticipated the development of Mexico into a large commercial center. Regarding its coming as highly desirable, they made speeches, talked to residents and strongly urged local officials to support the railroad proposal. Despite misgivings, the county court subscribed $50,000 to the project, provided the line followed the ridge route through Audrain.

Although some considered it "an enormous indebtedness," within five years after it was pledged in 1853 special taxes levied in 1855, 1856 and 1857 allowed the entire railroad subscription to be paid "without oppression or even inconvenience." By the time the North Missouri's 27.66 miles of track began to inch across the county most people were calling the appropriation a bold act by their officials and a brilliant stroke of luck for Mexico and Audrain.

Despite the approval of the ridge route, efforts to direct the line into the Mexico city limits were blocked when railroad engineers initially planned a route a mile to the north. It was taken straight through town only because of the public-spirited generosity of Dr. Nathaniel Allison, prominent Mexico physician. The owner of considerable property west of Jefferson and south of Liberty, he offered to donate the right-of-way through his land. This was enough to bring the line through town—a dubious honor, for although a boon to local business, it soon provided "the bumptious Jefferson Street crossing situation" that was to threaten residents' safety and peace of mind far into the future.

By the beginning of the Civil War the North Missouri, then completed to Hudson City (Macon), was operating one of the few railroads in the state. It played a major role in the management of the war in northeast Missouri, with Mexico occupied by Union forces to hold the line open for troops and supplies. Civilian use was temporarily limited.

During the early years of rail transportation, it took six hours or more to travel from Mexico to St. Louis. *Appleton's Railway Guide* for May 1864 listed fares averaging three cents per mile, "meals and berths free," with trains running every day except Sunday. Advertisements encouraged everyone to travel "Via North Missouri Railroad"; it could make connections with "the Great Salt Lake Mail, the Pike's Peak Express and the new Pony Express, which reaches San Francisco in eight days from St. Joseph."

After the war more railroads were built in the state, some through Audrain. The Louisiana and Missouri River Railroad, begun in 1868 with the county subscribing $300,000, soon became the Chicago and Alton, with lines through Mexico and a branch to Jefferson City. The North Missouri, financially troubled, became the St. Louis, Kansas City and Northern in 1872, and in 1879 the Wabash. The county's third trunk line, the Burlington, would come through in 1905.

Rosy predictions concerning the railroad's importance proved remarkably accurate. A major asset for the county, it brought advantages more and more apparent in the two decades before the turn of the century. Mexico, now called a "transportation hub," developed into a marketing center for a large area. Farmers had an easier way to sell crops, needing only to haul them to the nearest depot. Shops and stores, offering a variety of merchandise from St. Louis and the sophisticated East, attracted more customers and promoted a more modern standard of living. Businessmen and real estate developers began to see excellent profits as the population increased and the economy prospered.

The railroad would bring many celebrated visitors to town. One of the grandest was His Imperial Highness, the Grand Duke Alexis of Russia. He and his special car, on a national tour, left St. Louis at noon on January 11, 1872, passed through Benton City at 4:42 P.M. and reached Mexico at 5:00 P.M., making a brief stop so that the waiting crowd could catch a glimpse of the grand duke. Over the years there would be many other such visitors, including U.S. presidents.

Residents greatly appreciated the railroad. Before the development of the automobile and the radio, it was their main contact with the rest of the nation. With each arriving train the mystery of faraway places touched their Union Depot, and for many a restless soul the midnight wail of a train whistle stirred a longing to see the world at the end of the railroad track.

Old Ajax, chugging down the line back in the mid-1850s brought with it, from all points away, many an opportunity for Mexico and Audrain.

13

Antebellum Audrain

During the decade of the 1850s antebellum America struggled with emotions and events culminating in the 1860 presidential election, the splitting of the Union, and the onset of the Civil War. Missourians reacted passionately to the decade's developing issues: abolition, state's rights, popular sovereignty and secession. They also followed a long battle over one of their U.S. Senate seats and argued the fate of a young black girl in Callaway County accused of killing her master. Central to each issue was the institution of slavery. As slavery overwhelmed the nation during the decade, so did it also overpower antebellum Audrain County.

In the absence of other early records, the 1840, 1850 and 1860 Federal Census Reports provide many statistics about county life during these pre–Civil War years. At its first census, in 1840, Audrain's population stood at 1,989. Of these 1,722 were white: 890 males and 832 females. The number of slaves, or *Colored*, was listed as 267, along with six "free colored females." Over the next ten years the population rose only to 3,506, with the county seat still too small for a separate count. That 1850 census numbered only 3,048 white inhabitants and 457 slaves, with one "freed colored," a ratio of around 14 percent.

Slavery, according to one early county historian, was locally "more of a condition than a choice of the slaveholder." Audrain had no large plantations with numerous slaves. In this county of small farms slaveholding appears to have been the result of inheritance rather than a conscious, growing practice. Some settlers had previously freed their slaves, while a few brought colored people with them whose status blurred in light of common practice, since many were in effect given their freedom but stayed on as family servants. Some were even "rented out" for labor or specific tasks. Little official mention remains of their presence in the area; one 1856 Mexico city ordinance listed a punishment of "ten stripes on the bare back" against any slave for getting drunk within town—whether used or not is unknown.

Most slaveholding families lived in the Salt River Township, which included Mexico, with a good number in Wilson and Saling. Some listed only one or two slaves, while others claimed a dozen or more. According to 1840 figures, John B. Morris and his wife, with six children, owned ten slaves. The Virginia-born Robert Mansfield had two small children and eight slaves. James Fenton, the county's largest owner, listed one son over 21, seven children under 20 and twenty-five slaves. Among the latter were two males between 20 and 24, and eleven females under 24, with some living elsewhere. The Cardwell, Beatty, Muldrow, Clark, Willingham, Powell, Gamble and Sullinger families, among others, also had slaves.

Though circumstances varied, local owners appear conscientious in their responsibilities to their slaves. When Mrs. Malinda Sullinger, a widow, moved with her family from Boone County to Mexico in 1845, she gave "Uncle Isaac," her faithful overseer, and his wife and children not only their freedom, but also forty acres of land; in return he worked her farm until she could sell it. Her granddaughter wrote years later: "She thus put into practice her belief in the gradual emancipation of the slaves. She did not believe it right to sell her slaves, and took them all to Mexico."

A clause in the will of Edward Beatty, dated May 1847, stated that at the death of his wife, "if Aaron the black man is still living the property then falling back to my children from her must not be divided untill they make some permanent arrangements between themselves for the support of said negro man allowing him to make choice of which one of the children he will live with." If his wife chose to sell the farm, "in that case Aaron the black man is to be provided for before any of the property is disposed of."

Another story surviving the years is told about John P. Clark's strong young black man named George. No record remains of any slave auctions in the county, but traders on occasion came through and one was particularly taken with George, making several offers to buy him. Clark consistently refused; most residents considered selling a slave to be "inhumane." When the offer climbed to the very high sum of $3,000 Clark, always pressed for cash, finally agreed to consider it, on one condition: George was to make the final decision. The matter was discussed, George made it known that he did not want to leave, and Clark did not sell him. He stayed with Clark until the Civil War, volunteered into the U.S. Army, "made a good soldier," and returned to Mexico to become a productive member of the black community.

These antebellum years were, however, significant to the county for reasons other than slavery. In 1850, still thinly inhabited, Audrain listed 523 family units and 498 dwellings. A typical rural area, it counted 417 farms under cultivation and claimed only ten "industrial establishments," probably the stores and businesses in Mexico.

During the next decade Audrain began to emerge from the lethargy and isolation of its first twenty years. For the first time it showed signs of population growth, agricultural leadership and commercial progress. Where early settlers raised enough food and produce for their own needs, rarely having much to sell, now they began to grow more corn and oats, and to raise cattle, sheep and hogs for market. By 1860 conditions had so improved that the county was "beginning to be accounted one of the progressive agriculture counties of Northeast Missouri."

Several factors pushed the county into progress. Of major importance was the railroad, raising expectations of a booming trade. Also significant was the passage of the 1854 Graduation Act, lowering the cost of public land to only one bit (12 and 1/2 cents) per acre. A new steel-tipped plow made it easier to cultivate the prairie, encouraging its settlement. The incorporation of the county seat, first as the Town and then the City of Mexico, attracted professional men and merchants, who now could compete with the old river towns. "Progress thence forward and up to the commencement of the war," reads an 1876 account of Mexico, "astonished not only its rivals but even its own inhabitants."

The 1860 census reflected Audrain's growth. Its population had more than doubled over the decade, rising to 8,075, with Mexico, now warranting its own count, claiming 960. While not considered a factor in the previous decade's growth, the county's 1,166 slaves remained an important presence. Many residents, aware of the enormity of the slave problem, sensed trouble looming on the national scene and feared its effects locally. Along with others across the nation, they viewed the coming November elections with increasing concern.

In 1860 four men were nominated for president of the United States. The Democrats split, its northern faction running Stephen A. Douglas and its southern faction, John C. Breckenridge. The new Republican Party nominated Abraham Lincoln, while a strong compromise party supported John Bell. Audrain voters steered away from the extreme elements of both the Republicans (who advocated abolition) and the Democrats (who threatened secession) clinging instead to the more moderate groups. Two election poles were set up in the Court House yard, one for Bell and one for Douglas.

Interest in the election ran high. After months of speeches by secessionists, state's rights advocates and Union supporters, county voters reflected mixed feelings. They elected a secessionist to the state legislature and a Union man to the senate. In the race for president they cast 580 votes for Bell, 289 for Douglas and 206 for Breckenridge; only one man, L. B. Cudworth, cast his vote for Lincoln. Missouri gave its electoral votes to Douglas, the only state he would claim, and the nation elected Abraham Lincoln.

The antebellum decade brought to the nation political turmoil, shifting loyalties and uncertainty about the future. To the county it also brought growth and an entrepreneurial spirit that was only beginning to flourish when national events engulfed all else and Audrain, too, became "fraught with dissension."

14

Muldrow's Raid

No bugles blew a battle call that echoed across the Davis Fork of the Salt River. No gray-clad swash-buckling cavalry came cantering across the prairie, sabers glinting in the sunlight and flags unfurled in the breeze. No mention is made of an Audrain County battle in the *Official Records of the War of the Rebellion*. But in the long list of Civil War events that occurred in Missouri there is a note indicating a skirmish, at Mexico, on July 15, 1861. Military action, however small, did take place within the county that day—action due mainly to John G. Muldrow and his Audrain Rangers.

During the spring of 1861, as the Confederacy was being organized, Audrain residents faced confusion and indecision. Although a "strong secession sentiment" existed in Mexico, political allegiance was at first evenly divided across the county. While their state representative, Morton McIlhany, was opting for secession their state senator, Charles H. Hardin, was voting to stay in the Union. When President Lincoln called for enlistments to quell the uprising and bring the Southern states back into the fold, many of the county's young men, particularly those in eastern Cuivre Township, joined the state militia or enlisted in the Union Army. At the same time, when Governor Claiborne Jackson called for men to join the State Guard in order to "defend the state against invasion," many of Southern sympathy flocked to his side. Though Jackson failed to take her out of the Union, Missouri was represented in the Confederate Congress by Audrain's McIlhany—whose home county was occupied by the U.S. Army.

Audrain County was split—not cleanly into two pieces, one "North" and one "South," but haphazardly into countless fragments. One farmer professed loyalty to the Union, another down the road to the Confederacy. One Mexico home was deemed "federal," a next-door neighbor "secess." Some pretended one allegiance while adhering to the other. Many tried neutrality but finally had to choose. Suspicion, duplicity, false accusations and an undercurrent of distrust permeated the county.

The first indication of trouble came when a group of Southern sympathizers tried to run the Confederate flag up the pole at the Court House. A general fight developed in which no one was killed, but several were wounded. The secess flag never flew over Mexico, but secess tempers flared along with Union tempers and the rift that until now had been mostly verbal took on a different tone.

John G. Muldrow, though not involved with the flag incident, was a known Confederate sympathizer. A member of one of the county's oldest families and kin to others (a younger sister had married a Union man, John P. Clark), he was an avid secessionist. Though never officially organized, men who shared his feelings banded together under his leadership, calling themselves the Audrain Rangers.

Mexico by now was considered a strategic military site because of the North Missouri Railroad. Its control, allowing transportation of troops and supplies, along with control of the Missouri River, formed the backbone of the Union plan to keep the state from seceding. Because of its central location along the line, Mexico was regarded as the key to the northeast and was to be occupied by Federal troops, a fact causing no small concern for its residents.

In July, when word filtered up the railroad from St. Louis that six hundred of the Second and Eighth Missouri Militia were loaded on flatcars and headed west toward Mexico, the Rangers decided to act. Armed with makeshift weapons, they gathered at the edge of town, near the bend in the railroad east of the bridge. Hiding in the brush, they lay in wait.

As the militia train crept slowly around the curve, the Rangers attacked, wounding some and killing several. Caught by surprise, the troops could do little to fight back. By the time they realized their plight the damage was done and the Rangers had "dissolved" into the countryside.

In the aftermath of the skirmish the furious militia—mostly raw, untrained Germans who, said one observer, tended to take the whole war as a personal affront—stormed into Mexico. Intent upon revenge, they confronted frightened townspeople, even known Union men, threatening retribution, demanding food and damaging property.

Nor did they stop with destruction of property. At least four unarmed civilians were shot for no reason. Garland Surber had just brought a load of potatoes into town; when his horses bolted at the sound of gunfire, soldiers thought he was trying to escape and shot him. William Lockridge, on his horse and leaving town, became the victim of another "fatal shooting." On a deserted country road two men, despite declarations of loyalty, were stopped by militia; when asked their names and one said "John Q. Muldrow," they jumped to the conclusion that he was the Ranger leader (paying no heed to the middle initial) and killed him on the spot. His companion, also shot, lived to tell the story back in town, but switched his loyalties and joined the rebel cause.

A few of the Rangers made it back to their homes to remain prudently out of sight for several days. Some, among the estimated four to five hundred Audrain men to take such action, saddled their horses and under cover of darkness made their way south to fight with former Missouri governor Sterling Price, now a general in the Confederate Army.

Soon afterward, Union General John Pope, in command of northern Missouri, arrived in Mexico. Serving under him was Colonel Ulysses S. Grant of the 21st Illinois Volunteers. With three regiments and one artillery section under his command, Grant was assigned the territory from Montgomery City over to Centralia. Finding confusion and animosity in Mexico, the headquarters, he demanded stronger discipline, sensing that hostility among residents stemmed from the militia's disorderly conduct. He later wrote:

> I at once published orders prohibiting the soldiers from going into private houses unless invited by the inhabitants, and from appropriating private property to their own or to government uses. The people were no longer molested or made afraid. I received the most marked courtesy from the citizens of Mexico as long as I remained there.

The occupying troops set up "a small city" on the edge of Mexico, laying out dirt streets and drainage ditches in the fields at the west end of Jackson and Love Streets. Grant's tent, larger than the rest, was set up at the end of Depot Street, with his men "encamped in every direction from him except east." Only a few buildings dotted the area; to the north, at Love and Singleton, stood the six-room frame house of Captain William Gilliam, and to the south, the larger Clark home. Army headquarters were set up in a house at the northwest corner of Jackson and Water Streets, nearer the Square, while officers occupied several other homes.

During his three-week stay in Mexico Grant mingled freely with townspeople, stopping to smoke a cigar with some and dropping in for meals at the Gilliam and Clark homes. Soon ordered to Ironton, he was promoted to brigadier general and went on from there to win the war.

John G. Muldrow in particular had reason to appreciate Grant's friendly attitude toward Mexico. Tired of his outlaw status, the Ranger leader came out of hiding and, probably due to the efforts of his sister and brother-in-law, surrendered to Grant "at the house of John P. Clark." Neither punished nor held accountable for the raid, he took the oath of loyalty to the United States, swearing he would never again take up arms against its government—and kept the vow.

It was an insignificant incident and an insignificant group of men. But Muldrow's raid brought home to the people of Audrain the fact that their nation was, indeed, "rent asunder," their state divided, and their own county split. For her residents both blue and gray, it marked the start of four bitter years of war, an ordeal they would experience in their own way and a break which in the course of time they would also, in their own way, heal.

15

Audrain's Everyday War

$\mathbb{T}$ he Civil War in Audrain County was waged on a small scale, against backgrounds familiar and commonplace: a farm kitchen at dawn, railroad tracks by a cornfield, a barn in fresh snow. Ever on the fringes of the major struggle but not escaping its share of grief and heartache, Audrain's war unfolded amid everyday life, among ordinary people.

Several hundred of her sons, in both armies, fought at Wilson's Creek, Lexington, Pea Ridge and other sites, but not on Audrain soil. The county's sketchy war record centers on an occupying army, guerrilla warfare, and the railroad, in many ways the dominant factor in the local struggle.

Because of the railroad Mexico was occupied by the Union Army. Despite reports of better treatment during Grant's short stay, the occupation not only disrupted its routine but brought martial law, including curfew, to the town. City and county officials, forced to take "new and strange" loyalty oaths, were ousted from office and replaced by approved Union men. "The civil administration," wrote one resident, "was but the echo of military will."

People could not escape the military presence. Troops patrolled streets. Residents were stopped, harassed and at times arrested. The whole town suffered extensive property damage. The Court House was used to house soldiers and to stable horses. Some homes became military headquarters and officers' quarters. Other buildings were used as depots and storehouses. Even churches suffered.

At the small Presbyterian meetinghouse on East Promenade Street the occupation caused constant difficulties. While some churches, badly split, ceased regular services this congregation, many of whom were Southern in sympathy, continued to meet during much of the time. Early in the war Deacon James Pasqueth, who lived next door, often hid saddles and leather supplies in the church belfry, where at night rebel scouts collected them for Price's Army. One weekday morning when the church bell began wildly clanging, he knew "the wrong party" had found the cache and made off with the supplies. Though suspected he was never arrested, nor, in another incident was his wife, who harbored a wounded Confederate officer in one of the upstairs bedrooms and refused to allow a suspicious Federal officer past her front door.

Others in the church were affected when soldiers took over the building, removing benches, pipes and stoves and making normal religious activities impossible. Later, for reasons unknown, Federal troops also arrested a preacher and sent him to prison in St. Louis.

This despicable behavior toward a church so incensed a minister visiting town toward the end of the war that he wired the president of the United States, asking "advice." Clicking over the telegraph wires the next day came the following order to a U.S. Army colonel at Mexico:

> Vacate the Presbyterian Church. Replace the furniture as it was, and protect the worshippers. A. Lincoln.

This was done and the congregation was soon "worshipping as before."

Nor could people escape the impact of military acts. On one occasion Federal soldiers captured W. W. Macfarlane, the Confederate son of a prominent Callaway family, brought him to Mexico and placed him under guard. Army officials ordered his immediate execution. The next morning a distraught crowd lined up to watch as he was taken from the guardhouse, marched through town and placed before a firing squad. A coffin sat in plain view. Some even heard the "guns click." Only then did an officer step forward to read a second order commuting his sentence to imprisonment because of the heroism of a brother, an officer in the Union Army.

Although the federals sometimes patrolled county roads, they could not guard remote rural areas. Wherever possible Southern sympathizers destroyed sections of the railroad, burning bridges and tearing up tracks. The North Missouri was often impassable from Wellsville into Mexico and past town to Thompson. Infuriated by these incidents, Union officers issued an order holding anyone living within five miles of the railroad track responsible for any destruction. When men from both sides were arrested and imprisoned without trial, this only added to the turmoil. Authorities demanded payment from each county involved, assessing Audrain at $21,000. Suspected rebel sympathizers were forced to pay, while others innocent of involvement, who had even taken the loyalty oath, were also levied—"compelled to suffer," said one, "for the acts of irresponsible outlaws."

Throughout the war bushwhackers, Southern in sympathy and lawless in behavior, spent their vengeance upon many. Eager to fight but disdaining the discipline of the Confederate Army, these men declined to enlist, remaining in the community to lead vicious attacks on the enemy, or anyone they deemed the enemy. Early in the war Alvin Cobb, "a one-armed man," and his followers captured a Union officer and the mayor of Wellsville—against whom he held a grudge—on an inspection tour near Martinsburg; both captured were killed. Sometime later a group of bushwhackers headed by Littleby farmer Young Purcell raided the Columbia jail, setting free a number of Confederates (including Audrain men) and further incurring the wrath of Federal authorities.

Union militia were regarded by many as just as bad as bushwhackers. Ignoring the code of military conduct, they took the law into their own hands, killing and stealing as they chose. On more than one occasion a farmer, aroused in the middle of the night, was called out to his front porch to be shot or abducted by a band of militia.

Each such unlawful act was met by another from the opposite side, in an endless round of underground fighting. Although regular Confederates disavowed guerrilla warfare and Union officers disapproved militia tactics, such outlaws were seldom held accountable for their random killing. They appeared in neither civil nor military court. Suffering for the actions of both were the county's civilians.

Sometimes a truce was declared. When a daughter of the pro-Southern West family insisted on marrying an Iowa soldier, the war was forgotten for a few hours as the bride's Confederate relatives mingled with Union officers at a resplendent wedding feast at her home east of Mexico.

Much rebel recruiting took place in Audrain and rural northeast Missouri, where sympathizers welcomed a chance to enlist. On one such mission a recruiter with around sixty men divided them into small groups, directing them to nearby homes for breakfast. At the Peyton Botts farm a Federal scout riding by grew suspicious of the pre-dawn activity, accosted Mrs. Botts, threatened to kill her husband, and demanded information. When the "guests" arrived a short time later, they were attacked by Union soldiers. Though the rebel leader was wounded, all escaped.

At times Audrain residents were directly affected by events outside the county. On an afternoon in September of 1864 a train rolled into the Mexico depot bearing stacks of loaded coffins along with more details of the massacre at Centralia. Authorities, faced with the aftermath of Wild Bill Anderson's bloody slaughter, sent many of the dead to Mexico, the closest military headquarters. A few townspeople stood at the edge of the village cemetery on North Western Street as ninety-one rough wooden coffins were lowered into a single long trench on the far east side, "three deep, one on the other . . . right side by side and close together."

Not long after, in what came to be known as the Ham Brown Barn Massacre, local boys were killed. A Confederate officer and some teenage recruits were headed for camp close to the Audrain-Callaway line when several stopped to spend the night at the Hamilton Brown farm. Federals, tracking them across fresh snow, cornered eight in the barn. Expecting to be taken prisoner they surrendered. The next morning, however, despite the pleadings of a Brown daughter, they were lined up against the barn and all but one shot and killed.

As it did for the rest of the nation, the war in Audrain finally dragged to a close. Weary of conflict, her people marked the South's surrender so many miles away and ceased their own struggle. Wary of neighbors and of the future, many resolved to forget the war and its dreary litany of sorrow. Turning instead to the task at hand, they began to work for peace and, despite despair, to hope for better times.

IV

Not Wanting in Enterprise and Spirit

16

A Court House New and Elegant

At the end of the Civil War Audrain residents faced devastating property damage, discouraging business prospects and dismal economic conditions. A dreary reflection of the times was the deteriorating Mexico Square with its dilapidated Court House.

This small brick structure that for thirty years had well served the county suffered greatly from Union troops and horses, vagrants and runaway slaves. By the end of the town's military occupation, it had so disintegrated that no attempt was made to use it again for county business. Civic leaders, determined to forget the recent past and eager to get back to normal, were soon planning a new courthouse that would be larger, more modern and "elegant."

Construction of the building gave a much-needed boost to county morale. Begun in 1868 and completed the next year, it seemed a sure sign that good times were returning. By 1870, with former Confederates able to vote again and soon allowed to hold office, a new era had begun. The Court House represented a fresh start for all.

The cost of the building, after several disputes, was finally placed at $42,870.71. Of colonial architecture, the two-story red-brick structure had ten rooms. The front entrance, facing Jefferson Street, was framed by a portico and six slender white columns. Windows—tall, narrow and arched at the top—were outfitted with dark shutters that could be pulled shut against the cold, heat or glare. On the first floor were located county offices and on the second, a large impressive courtroom. Paneled in rich dark mahogany, it boasted high ceilings, rows of benches made of thick wood slats and an atmosphere of dignity suitable for the county's seat of justice.

The building's tin roof supported a cupola and high dome described as "attractive and substantial." In it were a heavy iron bell and an immense clock with four faces, one for each side of the Square. A special repairman kept them exact to the minute and made sure that the giant hammer struck the bell precisely on the hour, every hour. With its deep resonant *bong* the clock, audible across town, regulated the daily routine of storekeepers, businessmen and housewives. Farmers, in town on Saturdays, checked it to get home to milk cows; children, cautioned not to be late, counted its strikes to get home for supper.

A black wrought-iron fence and four gates, one at the middle of each side street, soon surrounded the Court House lawn. Hitch racks were installed at intervals for horses, mules and wagons. Rows of elm trees were planted, offering a shady refuge for visitors; flocks of sparrows, drawn to the trees, prompted desperate measures for bird control. Signs were eventually posted to keep ball players off the grass, promoting a sense of decorum, and in 1887 a granite marker honoring John B. Morris was installed, providing a sense of history. The stately Court House became a source of great pride to the county.

It also became a point of contention between the County Court, loath to spend taxpayers' money on mere cosmetic details, and the Mexico City Council, concerned with the appearance of the Square. The main problem for years involved access to the building. Irritated residents, fed up with wading through mud, demanded cross walks, preferably of flagstone, across the streets to each gate; the question was, Who would pay for them? Citing mud as one reason people did not pay their taxes, one newspaper complained that the "county court should either order a line of steam ferry boats, build a bridge, or put in new broad stone crossings to the Court House." When stepping stones were finally laid, the cry then arose to keep them "clear of mud."

Public opinion periodically insisted on repairs for the Court House, the fence and the hitch racks—often called an eyesore and finally banished a block to the north. Frequent coats of paint were needed, particularly for the roof and dome. Kept shiny and bright and usually flying the American Flag, the dome was visible from all parts of town and a few miles beyond—for anyone returning from a trip, the first sign of home.

At the completion of the Court House the county's population stood at around 12,000, with most people living on farms. Three towns besides Mexico, each on the North Missouri Railroad, had been established before the Civil War. Martinsburg, "beautifully situated in the edge of the Grand

Prairie" and first called Hudson City after a traveling clock maker in the area, had changed its name by the time its first lots were laid out in 1857. Benton City, first called "Jeff Town," was laid out in 1857, but had few settlers until after 1881. Thompson's Station grew up also in the 1850s. They soon became centers for farmers shipping their grain and livestock to market by railroad.

Immediately after the war there came into the county a number of families from Virginia and Kentucky, along with new settlers from Ohio, Illinois and other northern states. With the late 1870s and early 1880s came a further increase in population and the founding of several new towns. Some of these reflected the influx of immigrants from Germany, attracted by available, affordable land, better ways of farming the prairie and opportunities along the new Louisiana and Missouri Railroad.

Laddonia, at first a post office known as John's Branch, was in 1871 moved two miles north beside the railroad. Its two founders—Amos Ladd and Colonel J. J. Haden, whose wife's name was Donia—christened the new town Laddonia.

Vandalia, called "the eastern metropolis of Audrain County," was founded in 1871 by Colonel Aaron McPike. Farber dates to 1872. Both benefited from the new railroad and a nearby major highway, becoming centers for trade.

The early 1880s saw the growth of several smaller towns. Molino, north of Mexico, was named after a famous Mexican War battle fought at Molino del Rey. Rush Hill, laid out in 1881 in the middle of a flat section of prairie, got its name from its two founders, Gustave Reusch and Dr. William Hill. These along with the communities of Skinner, Rowena and Worcester reached their peak around the turn of the century.

Elected officials governing the thriving, prospering county now included, besides its three county judges, the circuit clerk, county clerk, sheriff, assessor, surveyor, treasurer, coroner and county school commissioner. Serving on the county court at the completion of the Court House and into the 1870s were Increase Adams, T. J. Marshall and John B. Morris, with B. L. Locke the longtime county clerk. John Gregg became the first recorder of deeds, elected in 1870 after this office was separated from that of the circuit clerk. In 1872 the probate court was established, its first judge being George B. Macfarlane and the next, serving for twenty-eight years, S. M. Edwards. Mrs. Clara Snidow, elected county clerk in 1898 after her husband died while running for the office, was the first woman elected to county office in Missouri; she completed one four-year term. All were staunch Democrats.

The business of the Audrain Circuit Court, with Judge Gilchrist

Porter presiding much of this time, increased substantially as the county's population grew. Almost all legal matters were handled now by attorneys living in Mexico, Samuel A. Craddock being the first, in 1852, to have opened a local law office. Soon joining him at the Audrain Bar were several who served at times as prosecutor: John Gordon, C. C. Ricketts and J. McD. Trimble. Others practicing into the 1870s, 1880s and beyond included C. T. Quisenberry, W. O. Forrest, W. H. Kennan, W. B. McIntyre, George Robertson, W. W. Fry and, senior to the rest, Charles H. Hardin.

Several Audrain County officials served later in the state government. Hardin became Governor of Missouri in 1875. In 1890, Probate Judge Macfarlane, instrumental in setting up the probate system for the entire state, was appointed to the Missouri Supreme Court, the first of three Audrain judges to serve on the High Court (the other two, much later, would be Circuit Judge Ernest S. Gantt [1927-1947] and Circuit Judge Frank B. Hollingsworth [1950-1964]). D. H. McIntyre served as Missouri attorney general, Sam B. Cook as secretary of state, Howard A. Gass as superintendent of education, and Eppa Elliott, after twenty years as Audrain Circuit Clerk, in 1930 became Clerk of the Missouri Supreme Court.

For all its eighty years this Court House stood at the center of county activity. Its bell was rung to notify the public of every important event: court sessions, fires, deaths of prominent citizens and any emergency. Along with trials, tax collection, record keeping and other county business, community events focused on it, with groups meeting there for many purposes.

In 1881, when "the bloody hand of the assassin struck down" U.S. President James Garfield, resolutions were passed in his honor by a group assembled at the Court House. Political rallies held on its lawn promoted such candidates as Aylett Buckner and Champ Clark for Congress, George Vest and James A. Reed for U.S. Senator and William Jennings Bryan for President. Speakings and picnics boosted local campaigns for, among others, C. F. Clark, E. A. Shannon, E. C. Waters, Rhodes Clay, W. W. Botts and Alexander Carter—all Democrats. Still later the Court House welcomed more campaigners for speeches and "handshaking visits," among them local candidates Suggett Edwards, Ralph Cornett and Georgia D. Irvine and, statewide, Lloyd Stark, Clarence Cannon, Bennett Clark and Harry Truman.

Every procession of any importance centered on the Court House. Independence Day parades, Flower parades, Fair parades, Elks parades, Victory parades and by the 1940s, Homecoming parades, passed by its front door. For many a Fourth of July celebration its portico roof, swathed in red, white and blue bunting along with the rest of the Square, served as a speakers' platform where officials and guests could sit in shady comfort.

By the mid-1930s townspeople gathered each Christmas to hear carols played on an organ as Santa Claus landed on the portico roof and tossed out candy to children in the crowd.

Wartime activities focused on the Court House Square. World War I Liberty Bond drives were held on its lawn. Missouri Military Academy cadets, in fatigues and carrying rifles, marched and even bivouacked around the building. Later an engraved memorial plaque listing Audrain men killed in this war was placed at the front entrance. In future years the public attended American Legion Memorial Day services and supported bond drives for yet another war.

Over its eight decades—from 1868 to 1950—Audrain residents developed a special affection for their dignified, elegant Court House. It had been an era of remarkable progress for the county, an era perhaps best symbolized by the Court House—and by its bell, steadily striking the hours and echoing across town.

Audrain Nobility

Among the newcomers settling in Audrain County in the dreary days at the end of the Civil War was a gentleman from Kentucky named Quisenberry. A wealthy farmer, sometime lawyer and recent widower, Colby T. Quisenberry Esq. quickly made his presence known. He talked money with John P. Clark, persuading him to sell his large home in Mexico. He talked marriage to Miss Emma Cawthorn, convincing her to take on his family of six children. He talked real estate with his neighbors, and to county farmers he talked purebred stock, choice mules and superior saddle horses. Mexico and Audrain County would never be the same.

His new forty-acre estate extended along Clark Avenue south to Breckenridge Street, along Breckenridge west to Abat, along Abat to Liberty, and east back to Clark. Its country mansion, built in the mid-1850s, was a two-story square frame house with front portico, four chimneys, separate kitchen and a central hall opening to two rooms on each side—a familiar pattern reminiscent of many homes in Kentucky. By the end of 1867 he had moved in with his new wife, two sons, four daughters and several servants, including a cook and her small daughter, and two "laborers." His new home he called Graceland.

Over the next dozen years Quisenberry held a position of high regard in the city and county. He opened a law office on the east side of the Square, "2d floor opp front door Court House," but a law practice was never his primary concern. He accumulated property. He became a director in local financier A. R. Ringo's new Mexico Savings Bank. He was elected to the first Mexico Board of Education, helping to build the town's first public school. He supported, as a stockholder, the reorganized Audrain County Agricultural and Mechanical Association, soon to become the Audrain County Fair. And he pursued his main interests in land and stock.

It was as a stockman that he preferred to be known. He brought into the county its first shorthorn cattle, Shetland ponies and fine saddle horses. His hogs ranked among the best and were sold to buyers in Europe. He bought choice mules, selling them on major markets in the South. His cattle were superior and he constantly aimed at improvement, paying any price for a good specimen whenever he saw one. He is credited with raising the standards for both purebred stock and blooded saddle horses in Audrain from "the merely good" to "the best."

At his new estate, to the northeast of the main house, he built a track and a large round barn made "almost entirely of glass." Here he held sales and trained horses. His Kentucky-bred American Saddle Horses, particularly the prize-winning Missouri Clay, attracted admiring crowds as they went through their paces. He urged local dealers to invest in good saddle horses, to breed them and to train them in the gaits so desirable in this horse-and-buggy era. He promoted horse races and horse shows. To him goes at least partial credit for the seeds of the saddle horse industry that would one day make Audrain "The Saddle Horse Capital of the World."

His wealth allowed a lifestyle that lent a vivid splash of color to Mexico. He made improvements at Graceland, adding such finishing touches as stained glass transoms. He filled the home with beautiful furniture, sparkling silver and fine china, in the front parlor placing a grand piano valued at a thousand dollars.

He and his wife entertained lavishly—more, it was said, than any family in the county. Dinners and parties were viewed as special occasions and the weddings of two of his daughters, one to her "Kentucky beau," were referred to as "notable events." Relatives and friends visited for weeks at the time. One small great-niece often rode a pony through the woods and along the estate's small branch, calling it "a fairyland."

When the family went for an afternoon drive the whole town stopped to stare. Their large open carriage, polished and gleaming, had painted on its doors, in gold and azure, the Quisenberry coat of arms. A coachman in uniform and tall hat perched on his high seat, reins in hand. The sleek and shining Missouri Clay trotted along smoothly, tail swishing, while Quisenberry, in his customary long black tailored coat, tipped his black silk hat to passers-by. Business on the Square ceased as clerk and customer stepped outside to watch. Mexico and Audrain County had never seen anything like it.

He stayed seven years at Graceland, in 1873 moving into another home on East Liberty. His health began to fail and on the advice of a doctor he spent some years in Colorado. He also began to suffer severe financial reverses. As one family member put it, "He came to Missouri with a fortune and spent it."

Contemporaries described Colby Quisenberry as "genial" and "generous," a man of "fine personal character" and "kindly impulse." He was seen also as a man who understood the "real nobility of life." It was perhaps this quality that most impressed residents of the county. They had little knowledge of, or patience with, nobility. But they recognized a good horse when they saw one, respected a good citizen and promoter of progress and held in healthy esteem a man who knew how to ride out in style.

18

Going to Public School

As the Court House clock neared the hour of nine on a typical morning in the late 1870s, many Mexico children found themselves scurrying along dirt paths and plank sidewalks toward the Public School. From blocks north and west they came, skirting the village cemetery and crossing the town branch; from the south, darting across railroad tracks and mindful of morning trains; and from East Anderson Street over to East Liberty, heading first toward the Square and then down West Jackson to Olive. No one dared be late.

Converging upon the school playground, a muddy cindered area enclosed by a ten-foot-high solid-board fence, they quickly joined classmates at the back steps. Promptly at nine the superintendent appeared, silence fell, announcements were made and delinquents were "admonished and corrected." With the aid of two boys beating snare drums, the student body was then "drummed" into school. Lined up according to grade and height, little ones in front, pupils filed into the building, down the corridor and up the stairs, each grade turning off as it reached its own classroom. The Mexico Public School, to the satisfaction and relief of much of the town, was in session.

The town's imposing first public school, built in 1873, represented the best of current education to pupils, parents, teachers, taxpayers and the local school board. First known as The Public School because it did not charge tuition, then as North Side School to distinguish it from a new school to the south, and still later as Central, because the superintendent and main

79

office remained there, it was to be a familiar sight to generations of children for the next fifty years.

During the late 1860s Mexico, like other Missouri towns and many rural areas, began to establish a system of public education. With a population of around 2,600, it elected six directors to the Mexico Board of Education: John Gordon, Dr. R. Bourne, William Harper, C. T. Quisenberry, Dr. W. Humphrey and Samuel Craddock, president. They quickly acquired the former Christian Seminary building near South Jefferson so that children could start school in the fall of 1870.

Regarding the seminary building as distant from the center of town and too far for most children to walk, the Board soon sold it for $3,500 and began to consider locations for a new school. A site at the northwest corner of Olive and West Jackson, two blocks off the Square and acceptable to most parents, was especially desirable. The four lots were purchased for $1,200.

The Board then paid $19,240 for the construction of the new school, described as a "marvel of a building." It had three floors, a basement, twelve classrooms, wide central corridors, steep stairs and outer walls sixteen inches thick. Contributing to the Gothic look currently popular were tall arched windows, a mansard roof and a tower. Classrooms were large, with twelve-foot ceilings, blackboards along three walls, and a raised platform across one end for the teacher's desk. Bolted to the floor in front of the platform stretched six or seven rows of desks with folding seats, slanted tops for better writing and, in an upper corner of each, an ink-well.

Behind the school, down toward the creek, sloped an enclosed bare playground divided by a fence—one side for boys, one for girls—with two small "privies" at the far end. Mud was a perennial problem; at the back door stood a broom that pupils used to clean their shoes before entering the building. Although the playground was covered with cinders and floors were oiled to control dust, the janitor often removed two pails of dirt from a room when he cleaned. Drinking water was drawn in a bucket from the well near the back door; several tin cups for the use of all sat beside it. With indoor plumbing, electricity and telephones still in the future, a prized feature of the building was its modern coal furnace with a radiator in each room.

The new school opened in the fall of 1874 with Professor J. C. Davis as superintendent, a half-dozen or so teachers and an estimated enrollment of two hundred. During its first few years it consisted of grades one through eight, along with a handful of upper class "scholars." By the spring of 1882 a full four-year high school was in operation, its location described as the third floor at the Mexico Public School. When Professor Daniel A. McMillan arrived the next year as the town's fifth superintendent, he came prepared to raise academic standards, continue strict discipline, promote the high school and attract more students into the system.

By September 1883, 658 students were enrolled. Records indicate that the enrollment increased to 807 by the end of the year: 387 boys and 420 girls. There were twelve teachers on the faculty, ten of whom were women, plus the superintendent, the janitor and Professor Treloar, borrowed from Hardin College to teach music part-time. Miss Lottie May, Grade 1 (at a salary of $47.50), listed 80 pupils in her class and Miss Spence, 72 in Grade 5. Grade 11, with 38, was the smallest class; Grade 12 had 48, only a few of whom would graduate. The average cost per pupil per day was eight cents, for a school year of 180 days. The average teacher salary was $53.71 per month.

Professor McMillan moved successfully in upgrading the school, maintaining the support of teachers and board and drawing goodwill from all parts of the community. Enrollment increased as higher academic standards became apparent, as more courses were offered, particularly in the sciences, and as parents relinquished a belief in the superiority of private schools; the public school system in many ways was soon viewed as providing a better education. Residents followed closely the use of their tax money and the progress of their school, often sitting in judgment at annual class exercises.

High school graduation exercises, held in the Kabrich Opera House, were the highlight of the school year. Most of the pupils, all of the faculty, many parents and a good portion of the population of Mexico attended the ceremonies. "It was a packed house," reported the *Mexico Ledger* on one such occasion, "almost to suffocation."

The Commencement Programme consisted of music by the school band, the invocation, the announcement of awards and prizes and an original oration or essay presented by each graduate, the salutatorian going first and the valedictorian last. The superintendent had earlier given board members a list of graduates, usually six to eight seniors, noting grades, subject matter, general average and class rank, along with evaluations in such areas as Society Duties and Deportment. Now in a formal petition on their behalf he stated: "I ask that these persons named above be granted certificates of proficiency in the courses of instruction and for good character."

Diplomas, made from sheepskin and written in Latin, were awarded by the president of the school board. For forty years this position was held by Mr. St. Clair P. Emmons. Thoroughly enjoying his role, he greeted the crowd and had a personal word—at times rather "discomfiting"—for each graduate. Each richly deserved congratulations. During these decades fewer than 10 percent of those who began the journey as wide-eyed first-graders would make it to the end. For this generation a high school diploma was, indeed, an achievement beyond measure.

To the graduates, Commencement brought a cherished moment of triumph. To their parents, gratification and high hopes for the future. And to everyone present, immense pride in this, their Public School and these, the children of their town.

19

The Governor
and the Grasshoppers

Audrain County has sent two of her sons to Jefferson City as governor. The first was the Honorable Charles Henry Hardin, the twenty-second governor of Missouri, who was elected to a two-year term in 1874. It was a term characterized by the adoption of a new state constitution, renewed emphasis upon law and order, efforts to "retrench" and strengthen the economy and progress in healing the rift still evident from the recent Civil War. It was also the term of the Grasshopper Proclamation.

Most Missourians had great confidence in this governor. His background and demeanor pointed to a man of integrity well equipped for high office. Born in Kentucky in 1820, he moved as a child to Missouri, where his family settled in Boone County. Regarded as "a brilliant scholar," in 1841 he received an A. B. degree from Ohio's Miami University. Returning home he studied law, opening a practice in Fulton. In 1844 he married Miss Mary Barr Jenkins, a member of Columbia's prominent Jewell family.

Over the next two decades he held several political offices, earning a solid legal reputation: Callaway circuit attorney, with a record showing that "no indictment he prepared was ever squashed"; representative to the state legislature, where he helped revise and codify the Missouri statutes; a director of the state insane asylum; and in 1860 state senator from the A-B-C District (Audrain, Boone and Callaway). At the outbreak of the Civil War he was the only senator to vote against secession, yet he was later disfranchised because of alleged sympathy with the Confederacy. It was at this time that he moved to a farm in southwest Audrain County.

After the war he opened a law office in Mexico, developing a "large and lucrative practice," and built a home north of town.

Nominated for governor at the Democratic convention in 1874, he easily won the election, being highly regarded as a man of "sterling sense" and "unimpeachable integrity." As the founder of Hardin College he was considered an educator and philanthropist. As founder and president of the Mexico Southern Bank he was viewed as a financier and businessman. Although not active in the Baptist Church until after 1880, he was always thought to be "a God-fearing man." It was with this background that he faced the "myriad hordes of grasshoppers" that attacked Missouri during his first months as governor.

It was to be a time long remembered as the "Year of the Grasshoppers." They had descended upon Kansas the previous summer, moving eastward into Missouri; farmers braced themselves for an onslaught the following spring. Hordes of the Rocky Mountain locusts had appeared before in the state, the first being noted in 1820, with others in the 1850s and again in 1866. But the destruction then was nothing compared to the misery and devastation of the plague of 1875.

Residents in Missouri's western counties spoke of "clouds of grasshoppers" that blocked the light of the sun. Landing upon a farm, they moved in "unchecked phalanx" across vegetables, grass and crops, leaving behind "only blackness." Children fought to keep them out of hair and eyes; some stood in amazement as the "brazen insects" ate strips of clothing off their backs. Trains were delayed as workmen cleared tracks clogged with crushed grasshoppers. They invaded houses, lay rotting in fields, dropped into wells and permeated the atmosphere with a terrible smell.

Farmers fought back by covering crops with blankets, digging trenches around fields and building huge fires, hoping to burn or smoke them out, but nothing worked. The loss of crops that year was estimated at over 10 million dollars. Said one survivor, "The suffering was great and the people well-nigh disheartened."

Governor Hardin was faced with the plague itself, the famine sure to follow and rising panic—the entire state, said some, would soon be covered with grasshoppers. In May he received a letter from an anonymous "Old Woman," who praised him as governor, likened the plight of the state to that of Biblical times, and begged him to set aside a day of prayer and fasting and to "request your people to humble themselves before God and ask Him to turn away his anger and thereby prevent the suffering of famine, which stares us in the face." After discussing the letter with his wife, the governor decided to honor the request. In talking about his decision years later, he remarked that he was not a Christian at that time, "but

I believed in the Bible, and I thought that God could remove the plague, and as Governor of Missouri, I ought to encourage the people with a proclamation to that effect."

His proclamation was issued on May 17, 1875. It set aside June 3 as a day of fasting and prayer "that Almighty God may be invoked to remove from our midst these impending calamities and to grant, instead, the blessings of abundance and plenty." The people and "all the officers of the State are hereby requested to desist during that day from their usual employments and to assemble at their places of worship for humble and devout prayer."

The proclamation was widely and genuinely observed. It also included a plea for contributions to people touched by the disaster; vast amounts of food and money began to pour into the afflicted area. On June 4 heavy rains set in, followed by a strong wind that began to blow the grasshoppers out of the state. It is recorded, too, that the next harvest was an exceptionally abundant one for Missouri farmers.

Across the state and nation, however, the proclamation opened a flood of controversy over the separation of church and state. It was to be one of three official proclamations by a Missouri governor to receive national attention, the other two being Governor L. W. Boggs's 1838 "order of extermination" directing that Mormons be driven from the state, and Governor Thomas Crittenden's 1881 proclamation offering a $5,000 reward for the arrest of Frank or Jesse James. Each focused attention upon Missouri and its governor, affecting the nation's view of the state.

After his two-year term was completed—and he chose not to seek another—Hardin returned to his "handsome farm home" north of Mexico. For the rest of his life, despite a long illness, he maintained an active role as an educational, political and religious leader in his county and state.

The Governor died at the Ringo House in Mexico on August 4, 1892.

The tolling of the Court House bell at nine o'clock that morning announced his passing. His body "lay in state" at the Baptist Church from Saturday until Sunday morning, when a memorial service—"the largest ever held in the city at that time"—was conducted at Hardin College. He was buried on his farm "beneath a pear tree near the gate in the garden." Two years later his remains were removed to the Jewell family cemetery at Columbia.

Charles Henry Hardin, Governor of Missouri and resident of Audrain County, is remembered for his political and philanthropic achievements—and for the grasshoppers.

20

Black Day for Audrain

$\mathbb{F}$riday, the fifth of March, dawned "rather cool" in Mexico. Within hours of sunup people were streaming into town from every direction, joining the "several hundreds" who the day before had arrived by train. By mid-morning more than two thousand outsiders jammed the streets, some milling around the Square, where they readily shelled out a few cents for a picture-card commemorating the day, and others heading east toward the creek. Reported the *Mexico Ledger:* "There never before was such a crowd in Mexico."

The proprietors of the town's two saloons had agreed to close for the day in the interest of public safety, selling no liquor. Ten extra policemen patrolled the business district and neighboring streets. An air of expectancy hung over all.

At the Audrain County Jail, on the south side of West Monroe across from the Court House, deputies readied a carriage, a wagon and horses. Sheriff Harrison Glascock, as directed by the State of Missouri, checked his instructions and prepared to do his duty.

Inside the Jail, awaiting the appointed hour, sat John Walker Kilgore. Sentenced for murder in the first degree, on this day he was to be hanged.

With Kilgore in his cell were his brother Alexander, who had spent the last night with him, and Father C. O'Leary, who the previous day had baptized him into the Catholic Church. Told earlier that morning that there would be no reprieve, the prisoner had received communion and then eaten breakfast. An observer describing his last day wrote that he "seemed to be very calm and collected . . . except occasionally when his eyes would fill with tears."

It was Audrain County's first execution. The facts of the case were few but, to the jury, convincing. On January 27, 1879, Lorenzo Dow Willingham had been found "on the stile-blocks" near a neighbor's house, with "right arm and chin shot frightfully away." Though obviously dying, he was able to speak, saying that Walker Kilgore had shot him "from the bush."

A few hundred yards away stood Willingham's wagon, "stuck in the mud, loaded with fodder." Nearby lay his hat and revolver, which had not been fired. Evidence at the trial indicated that the defendant had laid in wait for the victim, shot him once from the tree and, when he drew his pistol, "shot him fatally." The cause of the killing, according to news accounts, was a disagreement over "the hauling away of some corn fodder."

Kilgore insisted he was innocent, had been out rabbit hunting and shot in self-defense. When neighbors found him he even walked several miles into Mexico to give himself up to authorities. Maintaining his innocence throughout the trial, he later made two confessions, one implying that he was "a tool in the hands of others," the second admitting, in a confused signed statement, sole responsibility. A member of a family of long standing in the county, he had been born and raised near Skull Lick and was twenty-two years old.

The "long and interesting trial" was held in the circuit court of Judge Gilchrist Porter, with J. McD. Trimble the prosecuting attorney. The defense lawyer argued self-defense but was unsuccessful. The jury handed down a verdict of guilty in the first degree. Kilgore was sentenced to die by hanging on December 5, 1879.

The case was appealed to the Missouri Supreme Court, which affirmed the lower court, with the execution stayed until March 5, 1880. Over six hundred county residents, distressed at the sentence, signed a petition to the governor stating that Kilgore was a person uneducated, incapable of understanding "moral obligations" and "dwarfed in intellect." They urged that the sentence be commuted to life imprisonment. Governor John Phelps declined to act.

A proper legal document titled *Copy of the Judgment and Death Warrant*—handwritten in black ink, edged with black borders, stamped with black seal and tied with narrow black ribbon—was prepared by Circuit Clerk James Carroll and officially delivered to Sheriff Glasgow.

A scaffold was built east of town, and as word spread of the scheduled event officials anticipated a crowd of the concerned and curious on the designated day. By the end of that day the sheriff would fulfill his obligation and write on the back of the document:

Executed this writ in Audrain County Missouri this March 5th 1880 By hanging the within named Deft Walker Kilgore By the neck until he was Dead.

H. Glascock shff

$25.00   Audrain CoMo

After a long morning, at 12:45 P.M. Kilgore was led out of the Jail and seated in the closed carriage. Accompanying him were Father O'Leary and another priest, *Ledger* editor Robert M. White, Deputy Sheriff R. B. Hooten and Sheriff Glascock. Twelve special guards followed in an open wagon.

As the carriage made its way past the Square a swarm of men and boys surged toward it. A crowd estimated at three thousand surrounded the prisoner and his guards as they moved slowly down East Liberty "half way to the creek," turned right toward "the hollow just east of the railroad bridges" at the town's limits, and stopped at the scaffold.

"Not less than 5,000 persons," reported White, including "a great many women," packed the area. Some climbed trees in order to see better. Many watched from the railroad bridge.

At 1:10 P.M. Kilgore climbed the scaffold "with a firm and steady step" and "calmly repeated the Lord's prayer." At 1:28 P.M. the sheriff "adjusted the rope, tied his hands and feet, put on the Black Cap, and Kilgore bid them all goodbye."

At 1:29 P.M. "the trap was sprung."

When the deed was done, wrote White, "You could hear one terrible sob from the vast throng." The sheriff bowed his head and "though he is a man of nerve, we could see the tears trickle down his cheeks."

After thirty minutes the body was cut down and examined by authorities, placed in a coffin by his brother and the rope removed from his neck. Later he was buried "in the Barnett graveyard . . . beside his mother."

One month later, on April 16, at the same location and on the same scaffold, the county's only other execution took place. In a double hanging, Nathan Faucett and Jake Muldrow were executed for the murder of Octave Inlow. Afterward, all prisoners in similar cases were sent to the state prison in Jefferson City, with executions handled by the state. Commenting editorially in the wake of these two events White wrote:

We trust there will never be another hanging in Mexico. Thanks to the foresight of Sheriff Glascock, both of Audrain's executions have passed off quietly and smoothly without that tumult and excitement which generally attends an affair of that kind. We trust the lesson has been taught plainly in this county that the law must and will be respected. Parties appreciating this, there will be no need of hemp, and Audrain's scaffold will crumble and rot away with age, and not with wear.

V

The Growing Metropolis of the Grand Prairie

21

On the Square, c. 1880

The streets, labeled Jefferson, Jackson, Washington and Monroe, were of dirt, changing in season to dust or mud. The sidewalks, stretched haphazardly along the "mercantile district," were of planks, a foot or so off the ground and shaded here and there by wooden awnings. The business houses, some built since "the late War," were mostly of brick and stone, presenting an appearance of "good taste and culture." The Court House, reached by stepping stones across the bordering streets, was colonial in style, its shady portico serving as a convenient spot for loafing and its huge clock as the village timepiece. The Square at the county seat was, in the 1880s, the acknowledged center of government, business, politics, finance, shopping, news and gossip for the 19,732 residents of Audrain County.

On the Square were located a good portion of the town's "upwards of 80" stores and businesses. The oldest concern, on the east side, was James Pasqueth's saddle and harness shop. Occupying one of the oldest buildings—the one time Court House on the south—was Weinant's Bakery and Confectionery, which would in 1882 burn to the ground. One of the newer structures, also on the east, was the "4-Story Brick" of Geo. Leslie Ferris, "Dealer in Hardware, Stoves and Tinware," who set out to build the tallest building in town, topping by a few feet the Kabrich Opera House at the southwest corner. Reigning over the southeast corner was the sophisticated Ringo House.

The Square's shops and stores offered the finest in food, furniture, clothing, books, buggies, musical instruments, household wares and farm implements. Mexico residents and an increasing number of customers from across the county and surrounding area frequented them all for a variety of goods and services.

Most people had favorite grocery, dry goods and hardware stores. Families carefully considered which stores to patronize and who would then profit from their hard-earned money. Relatives associated with a certain store demanded allegiance and usually made the decision easy. Neighbors influenced the choice, as did the distance one had to walk and carry packages, church membership and one's business associates and fellow club members. Prices, while important, were usually not the deciding factor. People shopped their customary store first and if a desired item was unavailable, then felt comfortable going on to a second or third establishment; clerks even suggested where they might find what they needed. The customer was a thing of value; a store's proprietor tried hard to keep him and to please him.

Residents could find facts about the town's commercial enterprises in several sources, including the 1876 *Mexico Directory*. The 1884 *History of Audrain County* provided even more information, printing one newspaper's 1874 assessment of local trade, along with more personal information that "gives something of an insight into the character of the men who were then the merchants and tradesmen of Mexico."

The *Directory* listed twenty-one grocery stores. Several were on the Square, including P. Harding on the west, Bickley & Moore on the north, Fowler on the south and J. D. Morris on the east. With competition keen, they advertised staples (plain and fancy), sugar, coffee, syrup, fresh country produce, foreign and domestic fruit and such specialties as tea and oysters.

Grocer J. D. Tucker, "comfortably ensconced in his handsome new building, southwest corner of the square," enjoyed an annual trade amounting to "a snug $20,000." Barnes & Winegard's grocery saw sales of $200 a day, over the previous year taking in "fully $30,000." Other smaller markets served specific neighborhoods throughout town. Four separate meat markets, their goods in full view and dripping blood on sawdust floors, allowed customers to select their own meat and watch the butcher cut and weigh it.

Fashion was no stranger to the Square. Several clothing establishments offered ready-made attire from St. Louis, while "merchant tailors" provided custom service in cloaks, furs, coats and "gents' suits." Eight dry goods stores—carrying patterns and dress material, sewing supplies and notions, boots and shoes, household articles, millinery and clothing—flourished; one of these, Williams & Reed, was the largest business in town. Ricketts & Emmons, another "very popular dry goods firm," stocked for its customers an assortment of items including hats, shoes, gloves, groceries, hardware and Queensware china.

Several smaller millinery shops, all run by women, displayed the latest in laces, ribbons, corsets, trimmings, veils, hosiery and gloves, as well as hats. Mrs. Harding, an experienced milliner described as "one of the tastiest and most fashionable in Mexico," saw an annual business of around $2,500. She occupied "a modest suite of rooms on north side of public square," offering a "select stock of millinery goods, notions, hair goods and ladies toilet articles."

Other interests drew residents to the Square. Four banks handled financial matters. The largest and oldest—the Mexico Savings Bank, begun in 1861 by A. R. Ringo, who ran it for some time out of his pocket—was located on Jefferson at the southeast corner. Others were the Mexico Southern, the Mexico Exchange and the Farmers and Traders Bank.

More than a dozen lawyers, including the town's first, Samuel Craddock, had offices "opposite the Court House" (and presumably in the thick of things legal). A dozen physicians practiced from their second-floor offices, among them Dr. N. Allison on the north side, Pinckney French, M.D., "2d floor rear Savings Bank," Humphrey & Keeton, "2d floor nw cor Square," and W. W. MacFarlane, M.D. "over Llewellyn's Drug Store ws Square."

A half-dozen agents representing thirty insurance companies attracted clients, as did four real estate firms. Two newspapers—and occasionally a third enterprise of short duration—helped inform the public: the *Mexico Weekly Intelligencer,* J. E. Hutton, proprietor, and the *Mexico Weekly Ledger,* R. M. White, editor and proprietor. They voiced political differences and thrived on the common belief that controversy, real or contrived, helped sell newspapers.

Drawing their own faithful customers were three barbers, three billiard halls, eight wine and liquor dealers and eighteen vendors of cigars and tobacco. Also doing a good business were six drug stores, three jewelry stores, three bookstores, two "photo parlors," six restaurants and "but 2" saloons.

Not far away, off the Square, were four lumber companies, two undertakers, several wagon makers, two marble works, two icehouses, seven blacksmiths, two dairies, a gunsmith and three livery stables.

Going to the Square, which most residents did at least once a day, might entail picking up mail from the post office at the northwest corner, closing a real estate deal at the Court House, stopping by the Ringo for a cigar, picking out a shirt at Blum's Emporium or splurging at Llewellyn's on an ice-cold lemonade. Whatever the incentive, the Square in the 1880s was, for Mexico and Audrain County, the focus of economic activity and the core of community life.

22

At the Opera House

E ntertainment in early Audrain County centered around such activities as quilting bees, church suppers, political speakings and strawberry-picking parties by the light of the moon. Prairie towns like Mexico rarely saw dramatic troupes. Theatrical pursuits long remained homegrown.

By the late 1860s performances of some kind were being given in a small auditorium over a store on the Square and in a building near Liberty and Clark. Whoever the performers on this "kerosene circuit," they left behind no rave reviews. Many residents, particularly those better educated and more widely traveled, longed for more sophisticated theater.

Ready to provide a place for such endeavors was George Kabrich, who by 1874 was completing a new building at the Square's southwest corner. On the first floor was housed his dry goods store, on the third the Masonic Hall and on the second an auditorium measuring 44 by 100 feet, with a 20 by 30 foot stage and a seating capacity of over eight hundred. Available at once for "programmes," this was the Kabrich Opera House.

Mexico residents paying 10 cents, 25 cents and even $1 for admission, eagerly supported the theater. So successful was the venture that Kabrich was soon planning substantial improvements. By 1879 he had enlarged the stage, added dressing rooms, slanted the rear floor, built new galleries alongside four private boxes and installed over two hundred "elegant new opera chairs." Other refurbishments continued: replacing the drop curtain picturing goats and hogs with a new scenic drapery; a new upright piano; a better heating system; and, in 1888, for better lighting, the addition of two hundred gas jets, forty of which bordered the stage.

Theatergoers found everything "wholly modern."

The *Mexico Weekly Ledger* applauded the undertaking, saying it was "a great credit to our town to have such a tasty and comfortable place for amusements." Avid patrons of the arts agreed. Assured by the management that there would be no "smoking, chewing or eating peanuts" permitted, and that any "loud talking or skylarking" would be "set down on promptly," they frequently packed the house.

Mexico displayed its best for a night at the Opera House—especially its more dignified presentations. People donned their most elegant attire, ladies favoring "small black beaded caps" allowing a clear view of the stage. At least one gentleman wielded a much admired "gold mounted lorgnette." Eligible bachelors, warned to plan ahead and "secure her company now," attended with the ladies of their choice. Families brought out their buggies, at one performance a "string of carriages half a mile long" causing a traffic jam on the Square. Great excitement prevailed for a good show at the Opera House.

Around forty performances were booked each season. Since a moral touch was desirable to attract small town audiences, visiting lecturers were much in demand. Among these were Dr. Houser, who spoke on phrenology, the science of reading bumps on the head; Professor Henry, an expert on mesmerism; and the riveting Reverend Sam Small, whose lecture was titled "From Barroom to Pulpit."

Besides emphasizing the rising temperance movement, many speakers stressed what later would be called "positive thinking." In 1887 the Kabrich widely publicized the "Lecture Event of the Season," famed Southern evangelist Sam Jones and his inspiring oration "Get There."

For the appearance of *Christian Herald* editor DeWitt Talmage, called by some a "brilliant preacher" and by others a "sensationalist," guests from as far away as Jefferson City and Louisiana began arriving by afternoon trains. A large crowd applauded his speech, titled "Big Blunders, the mistakes made by men in this life." Reported one who was there, "a more elegant, refined audience was never assembled in the Opera House."

Concerts by soloists such as the "prima donna soprano, Miss Emma Howe," brought a good attendance. Hardin College musical ensembles, the Missouri Military Academy Band and student plays and programs drew full houses. Other orators and artists—"the best musical talent of this city"—were also scheduled.

But the main draws for the Opera House—their quality ranging from "matchless" to "tolerably fair" to "disgusting"—remained the traveling dramatic companies and variety troupes featuring singing, dancing, music and fast repartee. Some, such as Ada Stanley's Mastodon Minstrels, the "largest variety and spectacular organization on the road," drew mixed reviews; though sometimes favorably accepted, one year the curtain came down before the show ended, disgruntled patrons loudly regretting the absence of eggs and cabbages to throw on stage. Another production, called "the best we have had in Mexico for months," featured Miss St. George Hussey, who kept the house "in spasms of laughter." Other favorites were the Lillian Brown Jollities and Adelia and Maggie Bridges, singing twin sisters of great charm known as the Mississippi Prodigies.

Melodramas filled the Opera House from pit to gallery. *Uncle Tom's Cabin*, a perennial favorite, always drew a good house, but especially so the year the troupe announced upon their arrival that one of the play's largest and "most unmanageable" bloodhounds had gotten loose east of town. It took a search party and a "chunk of meat" to maneuver his capture, after which the show went on for an enthusiastic crowd.

The Golden Dramatic Company often played the Kabrich, the manager "booming" the sale of advance tickets and the *Ledger* urging a full house, commenting that "Few towns like Mexico are favored by such rare entertainments." Their popular plays, usually set for Fair Week, included *The French Spy, Lady Clare or the Master of Forges* and a splendid production of *Daughter of the Regiment*, pronounced by one admirer as "absolutely perfect."

Celebrated performers appeared. Future vaudevillian Eddie Foy drew local applause, as did the talented Cecil and Edna May Spooner. For the 1883–1884 season alone Fay Templeton (Fashion's Famous Favorite) was booked, along with Lizzie May Ulmer in *49* (The Most Beautiful Play Ever Written), Charles Gardner (The Funniest German Dialect Comedian in the World) and Patti Rosa (The Brightest Little Soubrette on the American Stage). A few years later, at one of the "most enjoyable entertainments ever given in the Opera House," the audience "laughed themselves hoarse" at *Muldoon's Picnic,* wildly applauding the star, Miss Whitney, who "was encored until she was out of breath but always came up smiling."

For over two decades theatergoers patronized the Kabrich Opera House. They wept copious tears for Uncle Tom and Little Eva, marveling at real ice floes on stage. They gasped in horror at Mr. Rochester in *The New Jane Eyre*, amazed by "One of the Most Realistic Fire Scenes Ever Produced on the American Stage." They whistled and shouted at jokes and songs, cheered heroes rescuing fair maidens and sighed their approval as true love conquered all.

Blinking at reality as they left the theater, patrons were momentarily refreshed—and occasionally uplifted—by the wonderful world of drama, suspense, romance and laughter that entertained them at the Opera House.

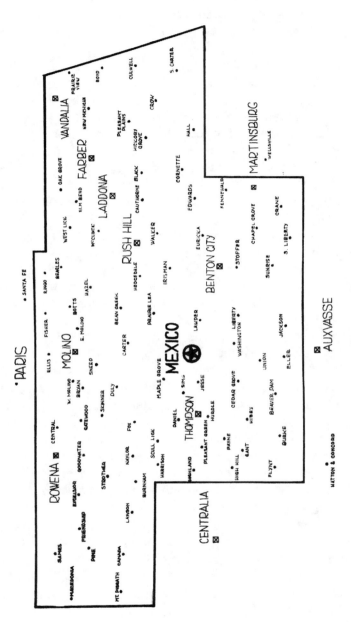

Map of Audrain County showing rural schools, circa 1900. Also identifies the larger towns in the county.

23

An Apple for the Schoolmarm

The residents of Audrain County in the years before the turn of the century began to take an increasing interest in education. While Mexico was building its first public school in 1873, residents in rural areas were also taking steps to make education available to all children across the county.

Since no child was to walk farther than three miles to attend school, the county gradually became dotted with small one-room schoolhouses. Each was under the control of a board of three directors; all were supervised by a county school superintendent. In most farm areas an acre or so of land for a schoolhouse was donated by a concerned parent, the land to revert back to the original owner if the school should close. Each school usually provided one teacher for all pupils in Grades 1 through 8.

By 1900 ninety-nine rural schools would be built and in operation at one time or another across the county. Besides the oldest, Union and Beagles, others open by the 1870s included Cornett, Maple Grove, Duly, Edwards, Washington and Dye. Among the largest were Cedar Grove, Molino and Lawder; the smallest were Chapel Grove and, with only four pupils, Sunrise.

Parents enrolled their children in school—whether country or town—confident that their particular school board would provide for them only the most commendable in curriculum, conduct and character. Symbolic of these high hopes for school, and the most visible representative of the educational process in action, was the schoolmarm. Coming under close scrutiny was every teacher in the county.

Teachers at Mexico's Public School on North Olive Street were typical of those across the county, the state and the Midwest. A look at their activities and the actions of the Mexico Board of Education provides a deeper understanding of the role of public education during those days.

In establishing a desirable educational climate the Mexico School Board performed a variety of duties, their supervision extending to every facet of the school program. Composed of six directors serving three-year terms, this board met during these years at the convenience of its members, at any expedient place: the county collector's office, the office of J. J. Still, Mr. Menefee's Store, Sallee's Book Store, or the basement of Ricketts & Emmons Dry Goods. Seldom was anyone else present except the superintendent, and wide was the range of discussion regarding school affairs.

Board members were trusted to handle school money in an honest and upright manner and to spend it only where deemed necessary. Expenditures for furniture, supplies and especially coal for the furnace were thoroughly discussed and decisions always made with their limited funds in mind. The public's main concern was the financial report, which usually consisted of one number. The treasurer added up all the money that came in, totaled all the checks that went out and, commented a later superintendent, "figured a remaining balance within one cent."

Even the curriculum and the choice of textbooks were often left to the discretion of the Board, sometimes with the aid of the superintendent. Once, when the high school American history teacher needed a new textbook, several possibilities were considered, the slant of such a book being of grave importance. One director strongly favored a text of 300-odd pages, 120 of which were devoted to the life of General Robert E. Lee. Much tact was exercised by all present to persuade him that another more unbiased text might be the better choice.

Salaries were controlled by the Board. Usually directors followed the recommendation of the superintendent, who discussed with each teacher her behavior, length of time in the system and how well she taught. All salaries were low. While the high school principal was preferably a man (and preferably married) most teachers were women and, as such, were paid much less. In Mexico during the early 1880s the average monthly salary was $53.71. The superintendent received $144.44 and several newer teachers $30.00.

Many of the district's patrons regarded the Board's primary duty to be the hiring and supervising of the faculty. Every prospective teacher was interviewed by the Board. Said one member, "I will never hire a teacher unless I get to see her." A successful applicant, almost certain to be a member's friend or relative, submitted recommendations, a photograph and records of her "accomplishments." She also answered a questionnaire about her morals, church membership and politics.

Once hired, though under close supervision, the teacher was in complete control of her own classroom. Formal discipline was a fundamental teaching concept and, in keeping with the demands of the Board, dignity and strict control were to be maintained at all times. The mood of the classroom was serious. Only occasionally and at special times did most teachers allow any laughter or free-spirited activity. Learning, they often said, was hard work.

Regarding the teacher's word as law, few pupils chose to cross her. Her discipline, however, though affected by her personality, was made possible mainly by "a mighty force in the office." There the principal or the superintendent, always backing the teacher, provided any additional support that might be necessary. If a student was sent to the office once, that was usually enough, but if a verbal reprimand there did not suffice, he was relegated to the basement for a whipping. Here the janitor kept a supply of switches carefully selected for the superintendent, who administered and recorded each "corporal punishment case"—ninety-five in a typical year.

As late as 1903, when L. B. Hawthorne arrived in town as the new principal at North Side (the name given the first school to distinguish it from a new grade school known as South Side) teachers still had remarkable freedom in the classroom. He encountered one or two who appeared immune to any administrative supervision. One maintained discipline by directing certain boys to shovel snow or cut grass, during the school day, at her nearby home—whether as punishment or reward was never quite clear. Another, known for her creative ways and "marvelous sense of humor," was unpredictable and undaunted by authority. She once hurled a piece of chalk across the classroom, hitting a perennial delinquent who was acting up squarely on the side of his head; thereafter inattention by her pupils was rare.

One teacher practiced what the new principal called "genteel blackmail." Any pupil of tiny, "bird-like" Miss Karnes who could run home at noon recess and bring back a hot lunch for the teacher or somehow convince "Mama" to appear at the schoolroom door with a hearty repast might be "specially favored" in her class. A piece of meat and cold biscuits were fine, but rating high marks were hot corn bread, green beans and buttermilk.

The Board's supervision of teachers did not stop at the schoolhouse door but extended well into the "outer environs." Regarded as models for the town's children, teachers were to be impeccable in appearance, demeanor and lifestyle. At all times they were to be on best behavior—at the store, walking down the street, at church and at any social event. If she had immediate family in town it was assumed she would live at home; if not, she was expected to stay at the nearby boardinghouse catering exclusively to teachers. The Board's constant vigilance was required to oversee the proper deportment of all.

Any difficulties with school regulations, written or unwritten, might bring a faculty member formally before the School Board. Miss Callie Towles, elementary teacher, made a brief appearance at its meeting of February 9, 1885. Asked if she were planning to get married, she readily confessed that she was. Reminded that therefore she could not remain a teacher, she promptly resigned. Members accepted her resignation along with an invitation to her wedding on the following day. In this action they were merely enforcing one of their many rules relating to faculty behavior: married women should not be teachers.

The schoolmarm was constantly being warned not to "overstep what was thought to be right conduct." The public—and the Board—long remembered an early incident when two young women clearly overstepped that line. One evening these teachers were down at the dining room of a local hotel—a situation in itself thought to show dubious judgment. When urged by other diners to "perform for the amusement of several men friends present," they hopped up on a table and began to dance. Word of this scandalous behavior flew across town. By the next day numerous parents were voicing shock and outrage. "Of course," it was reported, "the girls were discharged immediately."

In the meantime, the typical schoolmarm, in town and county, aware of her unique position, carefully monitored her every move. She sat up straight, behaved with decorum, paid close attention to the rules—and continued to bring to the boys and girls in her charge a conscientious and thorough education.

24

Dinner at the Ringo

$\mathbb{M}$any a group of friends enjoyed its cordial atmosphere and cosmopolitan cuisine, a taste of big city life. Many a cultural society and civic organization met regularly in its parlor. Many a sophisticated couple, dance invitation in hand, slipped across the second-floor bridge spanning South Jefferson Street to its ballroom. And many a tired traveler, dusty with train soot, settled gratefully into the comfort of its rooms. Mexico's Hotel Ringo welcomed them all.

Located at the southeast corner of the Square—"in the heart of the busy downtown district," as it was described—the Ringo House for many years was one of the most elegant hotels in outstate Missouri. "Few cities throughout the country," reads a 1913 article on Mexico, "can boast of a hotel so perfect in its appointment and so substantial in its general appearance as the Ringo." It was "favorably known" and "extensively patronized" by guests passing through town, visitors planning an extended stay in the city, "commercial men" doing business in the area, and residents across the county who felt a strong sense of pride in this elegant establishment.

Built in 1866 by A. R. Ringo—once known as Mexico's "walking bank"—the lot and-three-story brick building cost "about $65,000." Considered by many to be the finest hotel outside of St. Louis, it featured a large mahogany-paneled lobby, a formal parlor, a reading room, a "handsomely decorated" dining room and sixty "finely furnished" guest rooms, the most desirable of which faced an outside front balcony. First-class accommodations cost $2 a day, rooms by the week from $4.50 to $6.50, with the management in the 1880s claiming an annual business of $25,000.

Recognized as the largest, most comfortable and most lucrative "hostelry" in town, it was advertised as open at all hours of the night, with "active and accommodating servants." When proprietors closed it in the summer of 1878 for the first of many renovations and refurbishings, the whole town checked on its progress.

According to the *Ledger* it reopened with "nothing wanting, to complete the comfort and convenience of the guests." Besides suites reserved for permanent boarders, rooms "newly papered and painted" were available for "transient guests." New carpeting cost over $1,200, and furnishings, much of it described as "marble topped veneer," allowed for "tastefully decorated suites." A new washroom on the second floor, supplied with water from a large "reservoir" on the third floor, provided an up-to-the-minute facility for bathing. One gentleman, greatly impressed, commented that "the bridal chambers are beauties in themselves and make a man wish he could get married two or three times in a lifetime instead of just one, perhaps."

Hotel guests received royal treatment. Passenger trains arriving in town were met by attendants who guided visitors to the Ringo buggy for the short ride over to the Square. In the lobby comfortable rocking chairs— as well as strategically placed spittoons—offered guests a place to spend their leisure time.

On the hotel's street floor were located several stores catering to guests as well as town residents. The Worrell Jewelry Company, noted for its large sidewalk clock sign, did a thriving business, and the Ladies Toggery, its windows displaying the latest "big-city" styles, attracted many customers. On a lower floor beckoned the Ringo newsstand, a billiard hall, a barber shop and a "rather fashionable saloon"—off-limits, of course, to ladies.

Presenting a vista of starched white tablecloths, the Dining Room offered meals rivaling any in St. Louis. For Sunday dinner at 1 P.M. on April 24, 1881, guests chose from a menu listing, among other items, soup, veal, ham, fish, beef, chicken pie, corn pudding, tomato catsup, parsnips, assorted relishes, homemade bread, transparent pie, gooseberry pie, chocolate cake, sweet milk, green tea, French coffee, almonds and ice cream. Whatever the choice, the cost was fifty cents.

Despite the presence of new hotels in town and changes in ownership and management, the Ringo maintained its fine reputation over the years. By 1910 it was advertising single rooms and suites, with or without baths; hot and cold running water; steam heat; telephone service (in the lobby) and well-ventilated rooms equipped with electric lights. Its position of prominence in town never wavered.

To the town's dismay, however, on April 19, 1918, the Ringo House came to an end in a spectacular and devastating pre-dawn fire. Headlines in the *Ledger* read: "Thinly Clad Guests Flee From Ringo Hotel. Flames Discovered . . . in Rear of Hotel Building at 3 A.M. Fire Spreads Rapidly to all Parts of Building."

Fortunately there were no fatalities or severely injured. A hotel employee, "Dad" Jennings, was the first to notice the fire. "Bare-footed and partly clothed," he rushed through the building waking guests. With the help of Ralph Null, the eighteen-year-old night clerk, he guided all safely outside. The hotel, six buildings adjoining it along West Jackson, and the equipment and "fixtures" of ten stores were totally destroyed. The loss was estimated at $250,000.

A concerned crowd gathered in the early morning darkness as the Fire Company tried desperately to put out the flames sweeping the Square's south side. No strangers to such fires, some helped fight its spread, others offered aid to hotel guests and many helped remove items from nearby stores. Valuable jewelry from his store was taken by R. D. Worrell across the street to the Missouri Power and Light Company's walk-in safe; boxes hastily filled with fine china, crystal and silver were stacked inside the hall of the Court House. Its lawn and surrounding streets were soon crowded with pianos, victrolas, chairs, umbrellas, tables and other merchandise from the doomed stores.

Spectators huddled in groups around the Square, a few standing at windows inside the Court House. They watched first the Ringo's north wall fall into the basement, and then the front go crashing down on Jefferson Street. Despite the use of five hundred thousand gallons of water in eight different streams, and though firemen fought it "in a thorough and efficient manner," the Ringo burned to the ground.

For weeks its charred remains scarred the appearance of the Square. For years the vacant lot reminded residents of their grand old hotel. Genteel and refined, the Ringo House for a half-century and more had given a welcome touch of class to the thriving prairie city of Mexico.

J. F. LLEWELLYN,

DRUGGIST,

West Side Square,

MEXICO, MISSOURI.

Drugs, Paints, Oils, Window Glass

PATENT MEDICINES,

Fine Cigars, Tobacco, Etc.

Agent for COHOSH AND TAR.

AMERICAN POPULAR CIGAR.

25

A Drug Store for All Seasons

One of the half-dozen drug stores operating in Mexico before the turn of the century was the prosperous establishment of J. F. Llewellyn, located "1 d n Opera House, ws Square"—one door north of Opera House, west side of Square. For many years customers from all over the county patronized this gentleman's store, for a variety of reasons.

Primarily they came because of his large stock of drugs. People complaining of assorted aches and pains were usually offered one of the many patent medicines prominently on display. Foremost among these were tonics and restoratives guaranteed to build the body and strengthen the soul. Paines Celery Compound in particular fortified anyone feeling puny, Wells' Health Renewer helped those suffering from "weak spots," and Bucklen's Arnica Salve, at five cents a box, brought fast relief for cuts, bruises, sores and other complaints. Ailing customers, selecting from a large array of pills, elixirs, potions and liniments, found comfort in headache nostrums, liver renovators, blood purifiers, colic and cholera treatments, cough syrups and, for stomach aches, soothing "peptomized laxative cordials."

Those whose afflictions were more severe or who carried a doctor's order were asked to wait while Mr. Llewellyn retired to the back of the store to meticulously mix and measure concoctions of tar, snakeroot, cohosh (medicinal plants) and other ingredients into the desired dosage. Liquids were poured into brown, green or blue bottles, pills carefully rolled and counted, and powders sifted onto a square of tissue paper and folded into a small thin box. Each was given the customer with strict instructions as to use, and the prescription filed on the hooked iron spike that sat on his counter. "Prescriptions Carefully Compounded at All Hours," read his advertisements, and for years only Mr. Llewellyn, a "trained chemist," could fill them.

Medicinal cures, however, were not the only appeal of this popular drug store. When it opened in 1869 it became the first store in Mexico to sell gasoline and kerosene. Window glass and hanging lamps were on sale, as were paints, oils and varnishes. Ladies shopped for "druggist's sundries": fancy soaps, stationery, perfumes and "tooth, hair and clothes brushes." Gentlemen stopped in for tobacco and cigars. A growing number of patrons, young and old, sat down at the counter to order the combination of flavored syrup, carbonated water and ice cream called a "soda"—delightful refreshment on busy afternoons.

Some people dropped by to talk about the weather. For years Mr. Llewellyn kept detailed records of all area weather conditions, using a tall handmade wooden barometer, a large thermometer and an elaborate rain guage. Beginning in 1878 and for the next forty years, he served as Mexico's representative for the U.S. Weather Bureau. Patrons knew that any debate about the hottest day of past years could be quickly settled, just as any hint of rheumatism, verified by the barometer, might be eased with some new nostrum.

Many customers were attracted to the store because of its proprietor's interest in scientific exploration. It was this spirit of curiosity and devotion to "progress" that prompted his advertisement in a local newspaper in November, 1885. "The Celebrated **Electric Light** is in operation at my store on west side square," he announced. "You are Invited to Call and See It." Throngs of people came to stand and stare at a single bare "electric light."

Mr. Llewellyn was soon setting up an electric plant in the store's basement. Civic leaders, rejecting proposed coal or gas lamps for the town's business streets, now began to advocate his "incandescent electric light" for the Square. But his offer to the city for streetlights (to be lit only when the moon failed to furnish ample light) met with reluctance. Said Councilman J. J. Winscott, "I'm eager for electric light, but . . . where is the money to come from?"

Impressed by the Drug Store, now brightened on dark dreary days by electric light, over fifty businessmen agreed to pay five cents a night for each light installed in their stores and for four street lights on the Square. The *Mexico Ledger* applauded this proposal, noting that there was no money in it for Llewellyn and that "electric light machinery" was costly. Later, when the streetlights were cut off due to lack of payments, it chided the city fathers, saying that "The darkness on the street can almost be felt . . . This looks like a step backward and must be attended to."

With taxpayers urging light for safety and storekeepers demanding light for business, the city finally acted. In 1887 it agreed to "contract with Mr. Llewellyn for light." Reported a gleeful *Ledger:* "Light at Last. The Council Comes to Its Senses and Votes for Light." The whole town acknowledged a debt to its own scientific genius, J. F. Llewellyn.

People also frequented his small crowded store in search of books. For years, on a shelf in the back, they found a variety of books and reading material that he generously shared with friends and customers. In 1902, when the Andrew Carnegie Foundation began to provide funds for the building of public libraries across the nation, Mr. and Mrs. Llewellyn and Robert M. White of the *Ledger* took the lead in obtaining such a grant for Mexico, eventually receiving a gift of $12,500.

When the public library was officially organized a few years later Mr. Llewellyn continued to provide the store's second floor to temporarily house it and donated more than a thousand of his own books for its shelves. A small tax levy was approved to operate and maintain it, with Miss Esther Houston serving as librarian. He also provided land behind his North Jefferson Street home for the site of the building itself, which soon went up at 316 North Washington. The new Mexico Public Library opened in 1914 with Mr. Llewellyn, its first president, serving until his death in 1917.

For fifty years Mexico residents benefited from the presence of John Frederick Llewellyn. They valued his medicines and vast knowledge of chemicals, his books and his generous spirit. And they remained fascinated by the variety of attractions offered by this small-town nineteenth- century druggist, whose imagination, ingenuity and curiosity extended to all who crossed the threshold of his Drug Store.

John Bingle Morris and his wife, the former Julia Ann Shumate. Morris was the first post master, owner of Green Tree Tavern and was the county office-holder for many years. He is considered to be one of the founding fathers of Mexico and Audrain County.

John Pleasant Clark, above, was an early Mexico school teacher, real estate developer and he built Graceland in the mid-1850s. Clark served as the Audrain Circuit Clerk from 1845–1856 and 1861–1870.

The Audrain County Fair Grounds on August 4, 1892. Note the tents, ladies' parasols, suits and dresses.

Charles H. Hardin (1820–1892), Governor of Missouri
1875–1877. Founder of Hardin College. Political,
educational, financial and philanthropic leader.

Walker Kilgore. Convicted for the murder of Lorenzo Dow Willingham and hanged at a public execution held in Mexico on March 5, 1880. A disagreement over hauling away of corn fodder apparently lead to the crime. This was the first of two executions carried out in the county.

The Missouri Military Academy. Opened on this site in east Mexico in 1900 after fire destroyed original campus. Taken around 1902.

The Audrain County Court House, 1838–1868, was the first permanent Court House and was in the middle of the Public Square, facing east on Jefferson Street.

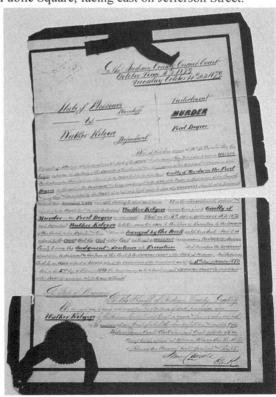

Death Warrant for
Walker Kilgore.

Audrain Christian Seminary, 1858–1861. This building was later bought to serve as the first building for Hardin College in 1873.

This is the East Side of Mexico's Square in 1858, as it looked before and during the Civil War, on Jefferson Street, looking south. The one-story building with the peaked roof on the left is <u>probably</u> Fenton's store—the first building in town. Note the fence around the Court House. Dobyn's Grocery was the two-story building at the southwest corner of the intersection of Jefferson and Jackson Streets.

Pupils at the Martinsburg School, 1890–1891. The teachers pictured are:
Professor S. T. Davis (in middle) and Miss Maggie Torreyson (front row, right).

A group of Hardin College students. Circa 1895.

Mexico Union Depot, around 1890. Located at corner of West Liberty and Western.

Trolley Car No. 1. This was a passenger car of the Mexico, Santa Fe and Perry Traction Company. The trolley was in operation from 1910 to 1919.

Waiting for a train at the Rush Hill
Depot around the turn of the 19th
century.

Time schedules for trains passing
through Mexico, circa 1890.

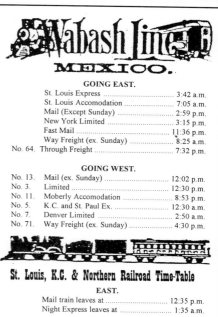

Wabash Line
MEXICO.

GOING EAST.

	St. Louis Express	3:42 a.m.
	St. Louis Accomodation	7:05 a.m.
	Mail (Except Sunday)	2:59 p.m.
	New York Limited	3:15 p.m.
	Fast Mail	11:36 p.m.
	Way Freight (ex. Sunday)	8:25 a.m.
No. 64.	Through Freight	7:32 p.m.

GOING WEST.

No. 13.	Mail (ex. Sunday)	12:02 p.m.
No. 3.	Limited	12:30 p.m.
No. 11.	Moberly Accomodation	8:53 a.m.
No. 5.	K.C. and St. Paul Ex.	12:30 a.m.
No. 7.	Denver Limited	2:50 a.m.
No. 71.	Way Freight (ex. Sunday)	4:30 p.m.

St. Louis, K.C. & Northern Railroad Time-Table

EAST.

Mail train leaves at	12:35 p.m.
Night Express leaves at	1:35 a.m.

WEST.

Mail Train leaves at	2:25 p.m.
Night Express leaves at	2:35 a.m.

Audrain County Court House, 1868–1950. The second on the Square. Taken around 1940, after the work projects of the Depression were done. View from southeast corner of Square. Building faced East on Jefferson.

Photograph of the east side of the Square, looking north, after 1934.

Audrain County Teachers' Institute, around 1895, meeting at Vandalia. In front row, second from left, Miss Jennie Karnes, teacher at North Side, later principal at Old McMillan Elementary. Front row, second from right, Miss Nannie Wright, beloved first grade teacher at North Side, recognized nationally as an authority on teaching primary grades.

Mexico's Public Square, looking at the West Side. Taken 1868, about the time the second Court House was started. Note the rail fence, mules, wagons, and horses hitched to the fence. Pictured are the furniture store, Commercial College, the general store, the saloon, Chicago Drug Store, a restaurant, the hardware store and a shoe shop. Commercial College was short lived. **Right:** Llewellyn Drug Store, "1 d n Opera House ws Square." Circa 1890. Note hanging lamps.

Below: The Ringo House, (or Ringo Hotel). Built 1866; destroyed by fire 1918. Located at the southeast corner of Square; front, with balcony, faces South Jefferson; side is along West Jackson St. (south side of Square.) Taken around 1900.

Tom Bass. Born 1859; died 1934. Bass was an internationally known horseman, trainer and showman. He was the friend of many leaders and trained horses for clients throughout the world.

Graceland. Built in mid-1850s by John P. Clark. This was the home of Colby T. Quisenberry, who brought improved, purebred stock and blooded saddle horses into the county. Photograph taken around 1890.

Hardin College girls in equestrian class. Around 1890. From left: Bettie Raymund, Bird Henderson, Myn Bast, Evans Ross, Neva French and Alma Peery. Hardin Hall in background.

Audrain County Court House and Square, late 1880s. Shows back of building on Washington Street. Note young elm trees, hitch racks and wagons. Street in background is Monroe on the north side of the Square.

Looking south down Washington Street from West Jackson corner. Circa 1879. Note store signs, dirt street, awnings and plank sidewalk. In the background is the Martin House, an early hotel.

Laying of the Cornerstone of the Methodist Church in 1902. In background: First Baptist Church. To the right of the Methodist Church, across Coal Street, was the Presbyterian Church. This intersection was known for years as "Church Corner." Although the present Methodist Church is still in the same location, the others have since moved.

East Side of Square, looking north, circa 1895. **Below:** Digging the foundation for the Mexico Post Office (the city's "Federal Building") at the northwest corner of West Jackson and Clark, in 1912. The Post Office operated in this building until 1967. Later, the building became the home of the Mexico-Audrain County Library. **Next page:** Mr. and Mrs. Joseph D. Morris' home at 928 West Love St. in Mexico. From left: Emma Ophelia Morris, Mary Garrett, Julie Calvin and Silas, the driver. (Joseph was a son of Judge and Mrs. John B. Morris). Taken around 1890. This house is still standing.

Mexico Board of Education, 1925. (Board that chose the High School site.) Front row from left to right: A. C. White; S. P. Emmons, president; and James R. Jesse. Back row: Theo J. Williams; W. G. Wilkins; and Charles Bledsoe. Emmons was on the board from 1879 to 1930, except for a few years, serving for a total of 40 years—much of that time as president.

Below: The Mexico Public School at the northwest corner of North Olive and Jackson. Built in 1873. Photograph taken around 1885, when the building was both a primary and secondary school. Note the solid board fence, towers, plank sidewalks and chimney. Later called North Side, and still later, Central School. Classes ceased in 1928. The building was sold and torn down in the late 1950s.

Allen Percy Green came to Mexico in 1910. He founded the A. P. Green Fire Brick Co. He was also an outstanding civic leader and philanthropist. Born 1875; died 1956. **Below:** Mexico Telephone Company switch-board operators, circa 1905. Located on the second floor of the Steinman Shoe Store on South Washington St.

Left to right: Dr. A. A. Wallace, long-time pastor of the Presbyterian Church; Col. Robert M. White, editor and publisher of the *Mexico Ledger*; and A. P. Green, president of A. P. Green Fire Brick Co. The three were good friends as well as leaders in all happenings in Mexico. Photograph taken around 1930.

Reception honoring L. B. Hawthorne at his retirement from the Board of Education in 1958. From left: Ross Ferris, principal at Hardin Junior High; Annie Bledsoe, principal at Eugene Field Elementary; Mr. Hawthorne, Superintendent of Schools from 1905-1912 and 1917-1950; Virginia Botts, principal at McMillan Elementary; Edna Dierking, principal at Hawthorne; and L. Buford Thomas, new Superintendent of Schools, (1955-1974). **Next page:** Sallee's Bookstore on the east side of Square, around 1905. On the left the Western Union Telegraph Office is visible. On the right is Dearing's Jewelry Store. The bookstore is at the rear. Note the stove, "palm tree," clocks on counter, hanging light bulb in glass, display counters and high ceilings. **Subsequent page:** Hardin College May Day Fete: The Queen's Throne. April 20, 1921. (The stage is in front of the first Hardin building.)

VI

A Progressive
Agriculture County
of Missouri

MEXICO FAIR

AT

MEXICO, MISSOURI,

AUG. 28, 29, 30, 31 and SEPT. 1, 1894.

Admission Reduced to 25 Cents.

SPEED PROGRAM.

First Day, Tuesday, August 28.

trot, 3-year-olds and under	$200 00
pace	200 00
trot	200 00
Three-fourths mile dash, running, for county horses that never started in a race	50 00

Second Day, Wednesday, August 29.

trot	$200 00
pace	200 00
trot	200 00
Mile dash, running	75 00

Third Day, Thursday, August 30.

trot	$200 00
pace, 5-year-olds and under	200 00
trot	200 00
Three-fourths mile and repeat, running	75 00

Fourth Day, Friday, August 31.

year-old trot (two in three)	$200 00
Free-for-all pace	200 00
trot	200 00
Half mile and repeat, running	50 00

Fifth Day, Saturday, September 1.

stallion trot	$200 00
pace	200 00
Free-for-all trot	200 00
Special for runners	

Entries to trotting and pacing races close August 22, 1894.
Entries to running races night before race.

✷ SHOW RINGS. ✷
OPEN TO THE WORLD.

Best Saddle Horse, Mare or Gelding, Guaranteed Stake, (closes August 15)	$800 00

Best stallion, any breed, with 5 spring colts (all considered)	25 00
Best mare, any breed, with spring colt (both considered)	25 00
Finest horse, mare or gelding, any age or breed, shown to halter	25 00
Best saddle pony under 14 hands	15 00
Best boy rider under 14 years	15 00
Best saddle stallion 4 years and over	25 00
Best saddle stallion 3 years and under	25 00
Best saddle stallion 2 years and under	25 00
Best saddle stallion 1 year and under	25 00
Best saddle stallion under 1 year	25 00
Best saddle mare 4 years and over	20 00
Best saddle mare 3 years and under	20 00
Best saddle mare 2 years and under	20 00
Best saddle mare 1 year and under	20 00
Best saddle mare under 1 year	15 00
Best saddle gelding 4 years and under	15 00
Best saddle gelding 2 years and under	40 00
Best saddle stallion any age	30 00
Best saddle mare any age	30 00
Best saddle horse, mare or gelding	100 00
Best mare any age or breed, shown to halter	25 00
Best harness stallion 4 years and over	25 00
Best harness stallion 3 years and under	25 00
Best harness stallion 2 years and under	25 00
Best harness stallion 1 year and under	25 00
Best harness stallion under 1 year	20 00
Best harness mare 4 years and over	20 00
Best harness mare 3 years and under	20 00
Best harness mare 2 years and under	20 00
Best harness mare 1 year and under	20 00
Best harness mare under 1 year	15 00
Best harness gelding 4 years and over	15 00
Best harness gelding 3 years and under	15 00
Best harness gelding 2 years and under	15 00
Best harness stallion any age	40 00
Best harness mare any age	30 00
Best harness horse, mare or gelding any age	100 00

For conditions or further information apply to Secretary.

W. J. BOTTS,
President.

C. F. CLARK,
Secretary.

FOR THE ABOVE THE

CHICAGO & ALTON
RAILROAD
WILL SELL EXCURSION TICKETS FROM

Kansas City, Louisiana, Cedar City and Intermediate Points

TO

MEXICO AND RETURN

AT

One and One-Third Fare for the Round Trip.

26

Come to the Fair!

Hot, sunny, summer days. Surreys, buggies and wagons. Clouds of dust. Rows of cakes and pies. Jars of gooseberry jam and cucumber pickle. Tea roses and dahlias awaiting blue ribbons. Giant red tomatoes and fat ears of corn. Crocheted doilies, knitted afghans and fine-stitched quilts. Picnic baskets of fried chicken. Lemonade. Cattle, sheep, hogs—and flies. Premium Missouri mules. And horses, horses, horses. This, once, was the Audrain County Fair.

The first fair, held at Mexico on grounds at the end of East Monroe Street, was organized in 1860 by the Audrain County Agricultural and Mechanical Association. Discontinued during the Civil War, it was reorganized in 1866 and again in 1880, when it was moved to a larger and more desirable site at the end of West Boulevard. From 1880 to 1899, and from the early 1900s until 1916, the county enjoyed an annual fair.

Members of the Association were quick to point out the benefits of such an Agricultural and Mechanical Exhibition. Besides promoting "higher ideals and new thoughts for every home," a good fair introduced new methods and new products covering the "whole circle of human industries." As a result farmers planted better seed, produced better crops, raised better livestock and built better houses. For both town and rural area the economy improved, the standard of living advanced and everybody took a new lease on life.

During the 1880s the Audrain Fair—"A Five Days' Exhibition"— grew steadily, with residents throughout the county strongly supporting its efforts. Among highlights over these years: displays of new farm implements; more and better produce; shows of improved livestock; a wider variety of horticultural exhibits at the Floral Hall, recently built and called a "thing of beauty and a joy forever"; an exhibit of handiwork, including a prized "silk and plush velvet hexagon quilt" of more than ten thousand pieces; shows and sales of Missouri mules; and "better and faster horses than ever."

Horses gradually began to dominate the Fair. Where, at first, farm produce was stressed with less emphasis upon livestock, the local group focused increasingly upon cattle, mules and horses. Cash prizes, ribbons and trophies were awarded for competition in saddle horse shows, pacing races, speed rings, harness races and the "2:30 trot—the biggest thing of its kind ever on a country track." As word spread across the Midwest, the Audrain Agricultural Exposition attracted more horses, more attention—and more people.

Visitors poured into Mexico for the Fair. In August 1888 the *Ledger* reported that "More people passed through the gates at the Fair Grounds Thursday than ever before in the history of the Association"—an estimated ten thousand. Many came by train; the Chicago and Alton ran special excursion cars during Fair Week from "Kansas City, Louisiana, Cedar City and Intermediate Points, to Mexico and Return." Farm families, forming a large percentage of the crowd, drove in from across the county and surrounding areas by wagon. Visitors and some townspeople rode the "nice conveyance" sponsored by a local restaurant out to the Grounds—"will call anywhere in town for you . . ." Others walked.

Mexico banks closed one day during the week, slowing down business in town and boosting the Fair's attendance. Children were admitted free on one day, ladies on another. With admission at twenty-five cents, many never missed a day.

Fair Week held an important place on the town's social calendar. Ladies assembled special ensembles for a visit to the Fair, particularly the major horse events, with newspapers dutifully reporting on their "fashionable toilets." On one day in 1881, "Miss A. W." appeared in a white linen lawn outfit with lace trim, on another in a black lawn with flounces. Other wardrobes featured a "Martha Washington suit in white," a peacock green lawn with shirred waist, a pale pink organdy, a black silk skirt and a "black plaid camel's hair polonaise." Gloves and parasols were basics for a grandstand appearance, and though a stylish hat topped most outfits, a small "hood for the head" called a *calash,* designed by a local milliner, was also popular. Gentlemen, despite the heat, wore jackets, ties, vests, starched white shirts and straw hats or black derbies.

Fair Week was not without its problems. One newspaper complained that the annual event, "as usual," would fill the city with "toughs, fakirs, thieves and gamblers." Residents were warned to lock their doors. Despite assurances by officials that no "gambling device" and no sale of liquor would be tolerated, wagers were made and a "plain drunk or two" sometimes seen. Occasionally, in spite of precautions, a runaway horse caused a scare. Dust prompted widespread grumbling; workers kept nearby streets and the grounds "well sprinkled" but could not eliminate it. Any complaints usually brought reminders that the larger the crowd, the larger the "receipts."

In its prime during these years and recognized as a vital part of the county's economy, the Fair helped make Mexico the "Saddle Horse Capital of the World." The Fair Association without question owed much of its success to the county's superb saddle horses; the saddle horse industry owed much to visitors drawn to the Fair. Horse lovers from far and wide came to see and to buy horses viewed as among the nation's finest. An observer noted one year that there were "four stallions that cost $10,000 in the saddle ring." A few years later the *Ledger* was reporting long ahead of time that "fine horses for the Fair are arriving by the score, daily."

The kite-shaped track built in 1892 further enhanced the reputation of the Mexico Fair. Many called it "the best half-mile track in the state." Allowing even greater speed and stiffer competition, it raised stakes to new highs and drew "the best horses from all over the country." Fifty-nine saddle horses vied that year for one $2,000 stake, with more than $14,000 paid in premiums.

Advertising "Every Day a Big Day and Every Race a Big Race," the Fair produced champion horses. Trainers and showmen rode winners named Old Montrose, Moss Rose, Black Squirrel, Rex Denmark and, by 1893, the incomparable Rex McDonald. World records were matched—and broken. Throngs of spectators, backing their favorites, packed the grandstand and lined the track.

Most county residents viewed the Fair with great pride and satisfaction. For many it was the culmination of months of hard work on entries and exhibits—a chance to win prizes and blue ribbons for a job well done. For everyone it was an occasion for pleasure and fun—an event eagerly anticipated.

Across the county, for young and for old, excitement ran as high as the soaring thermometer when the annual invitation went out to one and all: "Come to the Fair!"

REX McDONALD *833*
THE WORLD'S CHAMPION SADDLE STALLION
Campaigned over ten years, challenging all comers, without defeat.   A horse more widely known and beloved of saddle horse
admirers than any that ever lived
He is the sire and grandsire and great grandsire of champions
The Grandest Saddle Stallion the World Has Known
OWNED AND RIDDEN BY B. R. MIDDLETON, MEXICO, MO.

27

Champion of Champions

High on the list of Audrain County residents achieving national renown is the name of Rex McDonald. Of the equine rather than human variety of beings, Rex McDonald lit up the horse world like the new streetlights lit up Mexico. His career brought significant status to the Missouri Saddlebred, the permanent addition of "Champion" to his own name, and international recognition to his hometown, now called the "Saddle Horse Capital of the World."

He was by all accounts a magnificent horse. Jet black in color, sixteen hands high and weighing one thousand and fifty pounds, he was a high-stepping five-gaiter of "graceful animation." When he entered the show ring, body glistening under the lights, head alert and tail swishing in eager expectation, his very presence was called "electrifying."

In his prime he defeated all the great horses of the day, establishing himself as a saddle horse without equal. There never had been, said one who saw him, "a more perfect example of the saddle horse, the real simon-pure, original dyed-in-the-wool, blown in the bottle saddle horse than Rex McDonald."

In the years before the rise of the automobile many people kept a horse—or hired one from the livery stable. For short trips around town everyone walked, and for long journeys they took the train, but anything in between usually called for a mule or a horse, preferably the latter, to be ridden or to pull a wagon or buggy. A good deal of time, money and effort went into the development and training of docile, obedient, smooth-riding horses. An accustomed feature of everyday life, horses were a source of immense satisfaction to their owners, who took pride in their performance, stamina, appearance and bloodlines.

By the late 1870s a strong rivalry had developed between Kentucky and Missouri over the superiority of their horses, often proved in the show ring. The famed Missouri Clay, along with other local prizewinners named Royal Gold Dust, Artist, Montrose and Black Squirrel, brought much attention to Audrain, soon recognized across the state and Midwest as the center of the growing industry of saddle horse breeding, selling, training and showing.

When Rex McDonald, offspring of the prized Rex Denmark and Lucy Mack, was foaled near the Callaway-Audrain line in 1890, he entered a world acutely attuned to the beauty and value, both practical and monetary, of the saddle horse. As a new colt, described as short, "punched-up" and a poor specimen despite such fine bloodlines, he was at first a disappointment to all who saw him. But not for long. Sold at four months for $105 to R. T. Freeman of Mexico, he was carefully trained in the fine points of harness racing and saddle gaits.

By 1893, having claimed victory at several small shows, the promising young stallion was ready for his first appearance at the Audrain County Fair. Attracting much attention, he performed brilliantly, winning the $800 saddle stake—the highest prize then offered at any Missouri fair. Later that year at the prestigious St. Louis Fair, he amazed judges by defeating Lou Chief, Kentucky's renowned entry, and winning first prize. By the next year, when he won the $1,000 stake at the Mexico Spring Stallion Show, he not only was highly regarded by horsemen but had become a great popular favorite, winning every competition he entered.

Over the next decade he collected numerous premiums, trophies, stakes and blue ribbons, along with several owners. In 1894 he was purchased for $3,050 and taken to Kentucky as the highest priced saddle stallion of the day. Four years later he was brought back to Missouri by Colonel F. W. Blees of Macon, who paid $5,000 for "the best saddle horse in the United States." He was then turned over to W. D. Lee of Mexico to train and show. After he was bought (for $6,500) by a St. Louis gentleman, he was often shown by another Mexicoan, Bob Hisey, who kept him at his stables. Through all the changes, Audrain Countians cheered him on, always regarding him as one of their own.

With only six exceptions—and those because he was not properly shown—the powerful black stallion, "propelled by a heart of iron and nerve of steel," was undefeated over a spectacular show ring career. For several seasons he was even barred from all except championship competition.

Finally he achieved the highest honor of all at the St. Louis Fair in 1903, where he was crowned the Champion Saddle Horse of America.

His show days over, he was bought by a Columbia firm and retired. In 1910 Mexico trainer Ben Middleton, fulfilling a lifetime dream, paid $2,750 for the twenty-year-old. A few days later he proudly rode him in a parade around the Square. It is said that the great horse showed his real stuff on that April day, trotting, cantering, racking and bowing as a delighted crowd welcomed him home.

His popularity still rising, he spent the rest of his days in Mexico. After his death in 1913, his hide was stuffed and displayed in the lobby of the Ringo Hotel. When that establishment burned in 1918, he was rescued by firefighters and taken by Tom Bass to his barn. Here he was given his own special niche to the right of the barn door; countless children stopped by to see him and to hear tales of his glory days.

In the early 1930s the hide, somewhat the worse for fire and the passage of time, was removed from the barn and buried at the Mexico Fair Grounds. At the opening of each fair, the audience stood in silent tribute as a wreath was placed on his grave near the inside quarter stretch.

Later, when the Fair Grounds were sold for the site of a new school, his remains were moved to Plunkett Park. When that property was needed for still another school, he was moved across town to the grounds of the American Saddle Horse Museum. There a simple stone marker pays him tribute.

More than a century after his birth the legendary black stallion—this "aristocrat of the tanbark" and "royal blueblood of the show ring"—is still remembered as the perfect embodiment of the American Saddle Horse. The Champion of Champions, Audrain County's Rex McDonald.

Happy New Year
and many of them
1916

BELLE BEACH

THOMAS BASS

developer of

GAITED SADDLE HORSES

Mexico, Mo.

28

Blue Ribbon Gentleman

At the turn of the twentieth century Audrain County enjoyed a glowing reputation as the home of the perfect saddle horse; Mexico was called the "Saddle Horse Center of the World." Black Squirrel, Jack O'Diamonds, Forest King, Miss Rex and Rex McDonald were only a few of the Audrain horses to win top prizes in national competition and a permanent place among equine royalty. Guiding many of them into fairs and show rings across the nation was a Mexico horseman recognized as one of the greatest saddle horse riders, showmen and trainers in the world, Tom Bass.

The son of William Hayden Bass, a wealthy Missouri planter, and Cornelia Gray, his slave, Tom Bass was born in 1859 in Boone County. Raised by his maternal grandparents, he remained with them on the Bass farm when they were given their freedom at the end of the Civil War. His future would be directly affected by two aspects of life in mid-Missouri during these years: the difficult adjustment of former slaves into society and, in an age that did not yet know the automobile, the growing importance of the American Saddle Horse.

The saddle horse in the latter half of the nineteenth century was the center of a profitable and expanding industry in Missouri—and the center of Tom Bass's world. As a child he showed an unusual ability to handle horses and soon was riding, training and helping to show them at fairs. At the age of nineteen when he left home to go out on his own, he headed straight for nearby Audrain County, attracted by its superior horses.

Upon his arrival in Mexico he was quickly hired by the manager of the Ringo Hotel. His main job was to drive the Ringo buggy to the train depot to meet guests and escort them to the hotel, a task he performed with a flourish, driving the best-groomed and best-behaved horses the hotel had ever seen. Catching the eye of many in town, he soon was training horses for Joe Potts at his livery stable.

For the next fifty years he made his living from horses, buying and selling them, teaching young people how to ride them, boarding and training them at his own stables, and showing them in the ring. His love for horses was apparent. He always treated them with respect, never raising his voice, never working them too hard and never whipping them. The special horse-bit that he developed made life more comfortable for his horses and directly influenced the training of all saddle horses; though he never received a patent or any remuneration, the "Tom Bass Bit" was widely adopted by other handlers.

Except for a short time when he operated his own riding academy in Kansas City, Bass considered Mexico home for the rest of his life. Working for several owners at various local stables at first, he trained their horses and showed them at fairs across the Midwest. At a fee of thirty dollars a month, it generally took about ten months to produce a satisfactory saddle horse and a satisfied owner. Later he owned his own stable, his professional card reading: *Tom Bass, Developer of Gaited Saddle Horses, Mexico, Mo.*

Horses that he trained were soon winning blue ribbons not only at the Audrain Fair, but also in show rings across the country. Many he showed himself, over the years taking them to the St. Louis Exposition, where he won his first blue ribbon; to Kansas City, where he paved the way for the American Royal Stock Show; to Chicago's International Live Stock Exposition; and to New York City's Madison Square Garden.

By the 1890s he had acquired a national reputation for excellence as a rider, trainer and showman, an achievement remarkable in an age when some in the horse world were not ready to welcome a black man. Many recognized his exceptional talent, however, and were quick to say that he was respected not only for his ability, but also for his behavior, modesty and quiet manner. He was, they said, "always a gentleman."

He and his horses traveled in the highest of horse circles. He once was invited to London to show prize horses before Queen Victoria but declined, saying that he "wasn't much of a sailor and that the horses were worse." He rode one horse in the Inaugural Parade for President Grover Cleveland in 1893 and performed with others twice before President Calvin Coolidge. He and his horses, he once said, "jaunted around this country for many thousands of miles."

He made many friends, from ordinary folk to men of prominence.

Among the latter were community and business leaders across the Midwest, Missouri governors and U.S. senators and congressmen. At various times he was visited at his stables by future presidents William McKinley, Teddy Roosevelt and William Taft, as well as by William Jennings Bryan. Seeking his advice, they often bought and sold horses with his help. Some of his friendships were international in scope; in 1906, after he was injured during a horse show, the *London Times* cabled the *Mexico Ledger* to ask about his health.

Among the horses that he trained and showed were some that he owned. Though attached to several, his favorite, especially in the latter years of his career, was said to have been the world champion high school mare, Belle Beach. "Belle Beach," he used to say, "has more sense than some folks."

Tom Bass died in Mexico in 1934 at the age of seventy-five. Remembered as "America's premier horseman" and "this genius of horsemanship," he was mourned across the nation. Humorist Will Rogers devoted a column to him, awarding him a special blue ribbon. His funeral brought a large crowd, both black and white, to his home at 321 Whitley Street.

Nor was he forgotten over the years. In 1949 he was given a unique honor when the Missouri General Assembly passed a resolution hailing him as "a great Missourian" who "triumphed over his birth as a slave . . . to receive national acclaim." The Audrain Fair Association erected a monument at his grave in Elmwood Cemetery and dedicated its 60th Fair to his memory.

His hundreds of ribbons and dozens of trophies still remind those in the saddle horse world of the superior achievements of this internationally known horseman. For years mention of his name in his hometown brought recollections of seeing him ride, of standing in his barn to watch him train horses and, on occasion, of being invited into the Bass kitchen for milk and cookies.

He was, said one tribute, "the dean of American horse showmen and owner and trainer of some of the best horses that ever trod tanbark." He remains, for Audrain, the Blue Ribbon Gentleman, Tom Bass.

A FIRST-CLASS SCHOOL
For Young Ladies.

Hardin College, Mexico, Mo.

A. W. TERRILL, A. M., President.

Board and Tuition for ten months, $180.

Send for Catalogue.

29

The Halls of Hardin

On a day in the spring of 1873 Charles H. Hardin, Audrain attorney and future governor of Missouri, presented to the Mexico Board of Education a personal check for $3,500, taking the first step in the founding of "an institution of learning for the education of females" to be known as Hardin College. With this generous action he purchased the two-story frame structure built in 1857 as a private school and later used for public school classes, along with its surrounding five acres of land near South Jefferson Street on the outskirts of town. For the next half-century Hardin College prospered—and excelled—as an outstanding school for young women.

Governed by a board of thirteen directors and closely associated with the Baptist Church, the college benefited substantially from its founder, who initially contributed nearly $40,000 to the undertaking and before his death had doubled that amount. It also benefited from the generosity of the people of Audrain County, who enthusiastically promoted the institution, subscribing $7,000 for its first new building and soon adding $8,000 to its endowment.

Classes began in the fall of 1874. A principal and six teachers were engaged who took seriously their responsibility toward educating the ninety young females in their charge. Two academic courses were offered: the Preparatory, covering basic primary classes, and the Collegiate, covering advanced studies. Seventeen enrolled in the former, seventy-three in the latter.

Fees for the first few years were set at $15 for the Preparatory Course and $20 for the Collegiate, with $80 for room and board at Hardin Hall.

Additional costs included music, $20; German, $10; drawing, $10; and "Washing, per dozen, $.75."

Within two years the first group of advanced pupils was ready to graduate, having adequately completed the Collegiate Course. The first "certificates of graduation" were awarded in 1876 to Nellie Boulware of Fulton, Nannie Garrard of Centralia, Kate Wilder of John's Branch and Ella Forrest, Laura Clark, Ada Marshall, Mattie Craddock and Ella Hitt of Mexico. Representing some of the community's leading families, these young women established a pattern of excellent scholastic achievement and sterling moral values for the new college.

The county's new Female Institute, according to its catalogue, was dedicated to providing "thorough mental and moral training for young women." Its students could expect a high standard of scholarship and "wide-awake and energetic teaching." Besides daily class recitations in academic subjects, they participated in drills on penmanship, vocal music, drawing and the correct use of the English language. The administration demanded discipline in academic matters and stressed self-control and the wise use of one's time.

Much emphasis was placed upon the development of good character. Daily attendance at chapel was required and the highest standards of Christian living expected. Rising at 5:30 in the morning, the young women retired at 9:30 at night after a day characterized by thorough studies, appropriate reading, suitable food and regular habits. Seven minutes of each class hour were devoted to exercise, usually a brisk walk. Fears that "hard mental labor" for girls would "famish the resources of the body" were quickly laid to rest. Everyone was urged to concentrate upon learning and to avoid anything that "dissipates thought."

Clothing was to be "neat and tidy," free of laces and corsets and simple in style. No "finery" and nothing "expensive" or "extravagant" could be worn or displayed. For the first few years all students wore light calico dresses, aprons and white sunbonnets in summer, brown calico or wool dresses and blue bonnets in winter. Though bonnets and aprons soon gave way to more current fashion, uniforms of some kind were generally required.

Social regulations were strict and specific. Young ladies were not allowed to leave campus without special permission, nor were they permitted to attend parties, shows or the theater. Strictly forbidden was "company-keeping"—talking with young men. Although these restrictions eased with time, the college always stood *in loco parentis*—in the place of parents—with rules set accordingly.

Over the years teaching methods and curricula changed, with increasing emphasis upon the Collegiate Course of study. By the 1890s the institution was being promoted as the Hardin College and Conservatory of Music, "the Largest and Most Prosperous Ladies' College in the West." Enrollment had risen to 230 pupils, 155 of whom were boarders, with a faculty of 10 professors and 18 teachers from across the nation. "Sound and thorough instructions" were given in letters, arts, sciences, painting and drawing, elocution and oratory, modern languages, mental and moral philosophy, physical culture, stenography, type writing and commercial courses along with its special field of instrumental and vocal music. Its music department was considered unique and unsurpassed.

By 1901 Hardin would be recognized as the state's first junior college, with graduates granted advanced standing at higher institutions. Attracting students from Illinois, Kansas, Texas, California and the Indian Territory as well as Missouri, it maintained an enrollment of over two hundred and a reputation as "a highly superior small College."

From the beginning, trustees planned brick buildings for the campus. By 1875 Hardin Hall was offering a comfortable "College Home" rivaled by none. The chapel was soon built, followed by the gymnasium, the science building, a swimming pool, Richardson Hall, and in 1927, Presser Hall, bringing evaluation of its physical properties to over $600,000. By 1931, however, despite a large endowment intended to "last a thousand years," poor business practices, unwise investments and financial entanglements coincided with a nationwide depression that drastically lowered its enrollment, forcing the college to close.

Once called the "Queen of Western Female Schools," Hardin had become for women of the West what Vassar and Wellesley were for those in the East. Every year Mexico looked forward to the return of its students to campus, catered to its special needs, boasted of its many laurels and supported it in many ways. The town's shops, stores, schools, churches, homes and literary and cultural pursuits benefited greatly from its presence. Renowned for its musical performances, with the public often invited as guests, the college over the years had given the town and the county an air of refinement and sophistication that was both enjoyed and appreciated.

Audrain residents, many of whom had sent daughters to Hardin, deeply regretted its closing. Those living near the college had long grown accustomed to the familiar sounds of piano students at practice, hockey games in progress, a bell ringing for dinner . . . and on warm spring evenings, drifting across its shady lawn, the songs—and soft clear voices—of the girls of Hardin.

30

Gunfight on West Promenade

On the afternoon of July 10, 1902, in front of the Mexico post office on West Promenade Street, Audrain County's representative to the Missouri General Assembly, the Honorable Rhodes Clay, was killed in a burst of gunfire. People were stunned. "Astounded," said one report, and "caused to mourn."

Newspapers across the state reflected deep regret. Said the *St. Louis Republic:* "In the death of Rhodes Clay the Democratic party of Missouri loses a fine specimen of what it is beginning to need—young men of talent and highly educated ambition." From the *Jefferson City Democrat:* "In his death the State has suffered the loss of one whose talents . . . would have brought many blessings to the people." From the *Sturgeon Leader:* "The whole State mourns."

Neighboring towns expressed sadness. From the *Centralia Courier:* "[We] believed in Rhodes Clay, had faith in his integrity, and confidence in his ability. The news of his death did not create greater consternation in his hometown than it did upon our streets. Business was suspended and men stood about . . . lamenting the terrible event with husky voices and pallid cheeks . . . Had he lived he was destined to write his name on fame's deathless scroll." Said the *Laddonia Herald:* "The untimely taking off of . . . Clay was a calamity . . . he showed brilliancy far beyond the average Legislator, and not only introduced measures for the relief of the people but secured their passage."

The Audrain County Bar paid him tribute, saying that "In [his] death

. . . Audrain county and the State of Missouri has lost a faithful and able representative, the people a steadfast friend, this bar one of the brightest and most promising young members."

Rhodes Clay was born in Mississippi on January 19, 1875. The son of Colonel Green Clay, a wealthy planter, he moved to Mexico as a child. After attending the Public School and Missouri Military Academy, he graduated from Princeton University in 1895 and studied law at both the University of Virginia and Washington University at St. Louis. "Handsome" and "highly educated," with "the Kentucky flair for politics," he was admitted to the Audrain Bar in 1897, a year later becoming a partner in the law firm of W. W. Fry. In 1900, at the age of twenty-five, he was elected to the Missouri legislature. Recently nominated for a second term, he was considered "one of the brightest young men in Missouri."

Among his contemporaries was Clarence A. Barnes. Of an established, respected Mexico family and a few years younger than Clay, Barnes had graduated from the Public School and the University of Missouri, where he, too, studied law. Admitted to the Audrain Bar in 1899, he opened his own practice in Mexico.

The two young attorneys were often seen around town, at times in heated argument. Earlier in the summer "an altercation" over a lawsuit and related news articles had occurred between them at the Court House. Although both were arrested for fighting, neither was charged. It was at this time that Colonel Clay, aware that Barnes was usually armed, urged his son—"who was not in the habit of carrying deadly weapons"—to carry a revolver. Over the next few weeks the two men emerged as rivals in the courtroom, in politics (Barnes was a Republican) in society and even, it was rumored though later denied, for the affections of the same young lady.

Thursday afternoon, July 10, found Clay on the Square talking to a client, returning a borrowed umbrella and playing pool. Around 4:25 P.M. he stopped by the office of the *Mexico Intelligencer* (at the northeast corner of West Promenade and Washington, diagonally across from the post office), to pass the time of day with a reporter and Andy Winscott, a mutual friend.

Around 5:00 P.M. Clay stood outside the building chatting with Winscott, who invited him home for supper. He then ambled across the street to the post office.

By 5:10 P.M. he had been shot and lay dying.

The front page of the *Intelligencer* told the story:

RHODES CLAY SHOT DEAD.

Amid a Rattling Volley of Shots Clarence A. Barnes' Bullet Finds
Its Mark. Doubt as to Who Fired the First Shot—Barnes Wounded . . .

Representative Rhodes Clay is dead . . . Barnes' bullet, fired in the
midst of a fierce fusillade of shots from double action revolvers has
ended the bright young man's career. . . . Barnes got a bullet in the
right hand, fell, rose again and walked away . . . Clay was hastily
taken to Dr. Crawford's office . . . became unconscious, and died an
hour later.

The shots echoed through the quiet afternoon like firecrackers—which
many thought they were. Bystanders, turning immediately toward the post
office, saw two men, revolvers in hand, one fallen to the granitoid walk
and one staggering south past the corner. Witnesses inside the office described a meeting by the mailboxes, a brief exchange of words, the exit of
both men by the west door, and then a barrage of gunfire. Some said with
certainty that they saw Barnes fire first, "before the deceased turned" and
could draw his pistol.

Ten shots were fired. Two hit the post office window, two the
Intelligencer building, and one an adjacent doorway. Two hit Barnes in the
arm, knocking him down. Three hit Clay: one in the arm, one in the back,
and one in the right lung.

Winscott, walking down the street, rushed back toward Clay, yelling
to Barnes to stop shooting. Replying that "I have got no more loads," Barnes
turned up the street to his father's real estate office. After being treated by
a doctor, he was arrested by the sheriff and placed under guard at his parents' home.

Clay was helped into the doctor's office behind the post office. Friends
telephoned his mother to come immediately and wired his father, at a meeting in Joplin. He never regained consciousness and within an hour died.

By 6:15 P.M. the body was being placed in Lupton's undertaker wagon.

The funeral was held Saturday morning. Its procession, from the Clay
home south of town to Elmwood Cemetery, was described as "the longest
of any ever held in Mexico." Flowers and condolences poured in from
across the state.

The coroner's inquest, begun Friday morning, was held over until
Monday. On Saturday evening the body was exhumed and examined again
to validate claims of a third bullet. The coroner's report certified the cause
of death to be the bullet in the lung, "fired from a 38-caliber revolver, said

revolver being then and there held and fired by Clarence A. Barnes." Bond was posted at $10,000.

It is "a public calamity," said the *Intelligencer,* "one that is regretted by all of our citizens. . . . The Barnes family are very much depressed in spirit, and will ever regret the sad tragedy. The Clays, of course, feel that their loss is the greater. The community as a whole seems to sympathize with both families beyond expression."

But the community soon divided. Some felt that Barnes should suffer for killing Clay, others that he was innocent, shooting in self-defense. Some resented allegations about Clay's use of alcohol; others insisted he had been drinking. Some refuted the charges of premeditation against Barnes. Many upheld Clay's innocence. Two social sets formed, one with Barnes as leader, the other ostracizing him.

At the preliminary trial four physicians, the coroner and the under-taker testified that holes in the back of the deceased's coat and shirt were made by a bullet entering the back. The grand jury, said to be composed of several personal and political enemies of Clay, failed to indict—to the ap-parent surprise of the prosecutor.

Another grand jury was promised, but as weeks passed, none was impaneled. Despite repeated requests by the victim's father, the prosecutor still failed to act. Evidence from the preliminary trial was finally sent to the Missouri Attorney-General, who ordered the case to trial.

Other delays followed. A change of venue was requested. In the midst of this proceeding the circuit judge died. Three other judges were disquali-fied. Witnesses could not be found. "Insidious influences" brought to bear upon others were said to prevent their appearance. Attorneys, as the result of an election for a new prosecutor, switched sides. Newspaper reports were said to be "controlled" and the "luring bait of lucre or reward was held out on every hand."

The case went to trial at Troy, in Lincoln County, on October 19, 1903. The Honorable Nat M. Shelton was appointed Special Judge to try the case of *State of Missouri, Plaintiff, vs. Clarence A. Barnes, Defendant; Indictment for Murder in Second Degree.*

In attendance at every session were Barnes and his recent bride, the former Miss Ruth Lakenan, and their families. Also present were Colonel Green Clay, elected the previous fall to his son's legislative seat, and other relatives and friends of the deceased. Six lawyers were present in defense of Barnes; seven attorneys, including the prosecutors of Audrain and Lincoln Counties, represented the state.

The trial lasted five days. With the defendant pleading self-defense, there was no instruction for manslaughter. The verdict would be murder or acquittal.

After deliberating for one hour, the jury returned a verdict for acquittal.

To many the shooting of the "brilliant young Rhodes Clay" would always be, as the *Intelligencer* put it, the "Saddest Tragedy in the History of Mexico and Audrain."

VII

Constantly Forging Ahead

A CHILD TWELVE YEARS OF AGE CAN OPERATE THE MACHINE WITH EASE.

THE OLD WAY.
Expense of Washwoman, and clothes worn out on board,

THE MISSOURI STEAM WASHER
Save Washwoman expense, and clothes saved from

THE BEST WASHING MACHINE IN THE WORLD.
GEORGE D. FERRIS, Inventor.

Missouri Steam Washe

SAVES TIME, LABOR and CLOTHES

And does its work better than any other Washer ma

RETAIL PRICE, $10.00.

LIBERAL DISCOUNT TO DEALERS. ☞ **AGENTS WANTED EVERYWHE**

Over **FIVE THOUSAND** Sold during the Last Six Months, and every
Purchaser Enthusiastic in its Praise!

Absolutely no Wear or Tear on the Cl

31

A Little Wash-Day Sunshine

The household chore eliciting the loudest complaints a century ago centered around doing the laundry. "Wash-day," said one gentleman at the time, was "the dread of the family."

It was particularly the dread of the housewife. Current laundry methods involved stirring clothes in a kettle over an open fire and scrubbing them on a washboard in a tub—backbreaking, time-consuming labor for the housewife or the hired washwoman. Many women rose a half-hour early on Monday, the day universally set aside for laundry, in order to complete the task in one day. In Mexico, school for some years opened on Saturday and closed on Monday to allow children to help with the family washing.

But things were changing for the ladies of Audrain County, due to the efforts of a fellow citizen and his new invention, the Eagle Steam Washer. Perfected in 1883 by George D. Ferris, local tinsmith and hardware man, the new washer was first manufactured by J. W. Johnston and Company of Mexico. Also known as the Missouri Steam Washer, it cost ten dollars.

Demand for the new machine increased as rapidly as the average household's pile of laundry. Agents across the country reported phenomenal sales. At one point in 1884, the *Mexico Weekly Ledger* revealed that the company "sold over 2,000 washers in the last two days." By 1886 ten thousand were being produced every week, the *Ledger* stating that the washer had "proven a gold mine. . . .They have made thousands of dollars out of the machine."

The new washer consisted of a large metal kettle, inside of which was fastened a perforated tin cylinder with a handle. The contraption was placed on the kitchen stove, clothes put into the cylinder, water poured into the kettle and a lid fastened over all.

To operate the washing machine, someone stood beside the stove and turned the handle. Its special "miracle action" involved the use of steam, "the most powerful cleansing agent known to man." The contents remained in motion as the handle was turned, in order to "admit the steam to pass through the clothes freely, causing it to search out and eradicate every atom of dirt that lurks in them."

Advertisements proclaimed that the housewife would save herself time, labor and double the cost of the machine in a year. Since clothes received no wear and tear, white clothes and the "most delicate lace" could be safely washed in it. The heaviest blankets and "even carpets" would be easily cleaned by its special action. So simple to operate that even a child could do it "with ease," the average item took from eight to twenty minutes to get clean.

Husbands were urged to purchase them as gifts for their wives, for it would directly benefit their health. Read one ad: "Make your wife a nice Christmas present. Buy her a *Missouri Steam Washer*—only $10.00—and it will save many doctor's bills."

Praise waxed high for the "Best Washing Machine on the Face of the Earth." The proprietor of the Ringo Hotel noted that it would wash five to eight hundred pieces of linen per day, doing the work of three to five washwomen; he would not be without one. "Ladies governed by reason, not prejudice, will use it," said another pleased customer. And, declared Mrs. Kate Ferris, "One hundred dollars would not buy mine if I could not get another."

George Ferris, basking in the extraordinary success of his *Eagle Steam Washer,* soon turned to other projects. The Johnston Company, with dollars pouring in, moved from Mexico to a larger city. And, relieved of some drudgery, Audrain County housewives beamed at a ray of sunshine in the midst of age-old washday blues.

32

Hail to Thee, McMillan!

Students entered the doors of Mexico's McMillan High School for the first time to the sound of drums beating and trumpets blaring. On that early spring morning in 1908 they had assembled as usual at North Side School, gathered up books and anything else they could carry, and lined up behind the school band for a "Grand Triumphant Parade" around the Square. Much of the town turned out to watch as the student body marched up West Jackson, over to Monroe, and east two blocks to the new high school. With formal classes not scheduled until the next day, everyone assembled for a program of "speeches, songs and cheers." Said their superintendent, L. B. Hawthorne, "Jubilation and delight filled us all."

The students and the town had good reason to celebrate. A hard campaign had been waged, against "intelligent opposition," to convince the district's six thousand residents of the need for a new school. Professor D. A. McMillan, the previous superintendent, had personally persuaded most voters to pass a bond issue for $90,000—an incredibly high sum for a city like Mexico. The additional funds would allow, among other improvements, the building of a modern new high school. This, argued Mr. McMillan, was an absolute necessity for the education of their children. A half-century later civic leaders would still give him credit for unerring foresight and effective persuasion, one saying that "Mr. McMillan influenced the people of Mexico to vote a bond issue that became the foundation of the excellent public school system we have today."

Professor McMillan was regarded as one of the county's most beloved citizens. When he was taken ill and died before the completion of the new building, a grateful community named the high school in his honor. Said the *Ledger*, paying him tribute for twenty-four years of educational leadership, "It is the fortune of few men to be as universally loved and respected as was the late Daniel A. McMillan."

From 1908 to 1928 McMillan High School served the students of Mexico as well as many from the county's rural schools, always a proud presence in town. An increasing number of graduates of the county's one-room schoolhouses enrolled in the new school, paying around $60 a year in tuition. Some boarded with friends during the week or stayed with relatives in town, while others came in daily by horse and buggy or the trolley. With more space now to accommodate them, the high school welcomed them all, in many cases winning their allegiance as they joined town students in excelling at academics, sports and other activities.

Chosen as the site for the new school were lots in the east half of block 19, Original Town, with the front entrance to face Monroe Street. Along the west half of this 200 block were residences whose lots later would become part of the school playground. A local builder was given the $35,180 contract, the Mexico Brick Company supplied all brick except the facing, and local firms handled the plumbing and ventilating systems. The three-story red-brick building with white trim was a handsome addition to a street already lined with fine homes. Newspapers called it *The New Mexico $50,000 High School.*

To students, teachers, parents and administrators the new high school seemed an educational dream come true. Its library, large classrooms, two science laboratories and combination gymnasium-auditorium drew much praise. Although the third floor was temporarily left unfinished in order to save money, space was available for classes in home economics, manual training, vocational agriculture and other new subjects. The broad stairs, big windows, rest rooms and modern ventilation and heating systems provided the ideal modern school environment.

Matching its first-class physical facilities was a superior academic program. In its first year McMillan was named a standard accredited high school by the Missouri Department of Education—the second in the state so honored. In the same year it was also recognized by the North Central Association of Secondary Schools and Colleges, being one of only six high schools in Missouri so distinguished and only the second outstate school to win this recognition.

Students were taught by a faculty devoted to their intellectual development. Several of its teachers held the full Bachelor of Arts degree; all had at least the Bachelor of Science. Ten faculty members, all women except one, followed Superintendent Hawthorne and Principal Rolla B. Finley into the new school. Among its outstanding teachers over the next two decades were Miss Benson Botts for history and English, Miss Elizabeth Gill for mathematics, Miss Maude Orita Wallace for vocal music, Miss Lucy Denham for Latin, J. T. Angus for athletics and, for vocational agriculture, Alphonse Gorrell.

These teachers were encouraged to consider the moral, ethical and social development of their pupils as no less important than their "mental discipline." In *The Course of Study and Rules and Regulations of the Mexico Public Schools* compiled by Mr. Hawthorne in 1908, high expectations were outlined for the teachers: "By precept and becoming example, they shall endeavor to instill habits of social refinement, cleanliness, neatness, order, truth, purity, justice, honor, humanity, courage, politeness, temperance, industry, energy, promptitude, patriotism, self-control, and charity." Some of the best did just that.

A variety of extracurricular activities filled after-school hours for students. The yearbook was published after 1909. The orchestra, the quartette and the debating club prospered. A drama club presented such favorites as *Seventeen* and *The Beau of Bath*. For every performance, of whatever group, parents and townspeople faithfully provided an enthusiastic audience.

Sports became an increasingly important activity, igniting a competitive spirit eager to fight for Mexico. Fourteen boys were now on the football team. Described by the newspaper as not as "ponderous" as might be desired but "fleet of foot," they practiced on Woodlawn Hill or over on the field near Eastholm Street. By 1910 a mascot patterned after the school's "gentle canine friend" named Shimmie had made his appearance in the form of the Mexico Bulldog.

Basketball became more and more popular. Spectators filled the new gymnasium to cheer on championship teams. While several left behind excellent records, the 1915–1916 team was exceptional, being undefeated and listing stunning victories over Jefferson City (70–6, 70–12), Hannibal (60–15) and Ferguson (78–14). Coach E. E. Rich led such outstanding players as Ryland Rodes, Sam Locke, Bryan Atchison, Eric Cunningham and Joy Kistler to an unofficial state championship.

A girls' basketball team was also organized. Its first opponents were Hardin College and Marshall High School, with the team traveling to and from away games by train. After each game both teams enjoyed refreshments at a get-together hosted by the home school.

A high standard of behavior was expected of all students. Discipline was strict and rules readily enforced. Most students caught misbehaving were kept after school in detention hall, with extra homework and special written tasks also assigned as punishment. Occasionally a paddling was administered by principal or superintendent. "Saluting Minerva" became one familiar punishment as delinquents were banished to the school's main hall to stand in embarrassed silence before a statue of Minerva, the Roman goddess of wisdom.

Pranks and practical jokes were frequent. On one dark night a group of boys scaled the school's outside wall to the second story, hoisting into the corner classroom one protesting, frightened sheep. Left to graze upon test papers and history books all night, the sheep and a scene of chaos greeted an astonished teacher the next morning. An angry principal and an even angrier but determined superintendent lined up every boy in school for questioning, detecting the culprits by bits of white wool still clinging to dark socks and trousers. All were seniors. Most gamely took their punishment—which included cleaning up the mess—except for one unrepentant participant, who refused to accept responsibility and as a result did not graduate.

Over these two decades 1,323 graduates passed through McMillan's doors:

Annie Bledsoe . . . Turner Williams . . . Nesbit Livingston . . . Edna Bickley . . . Alan Coatsworth . . . Joy Kistler . . . Sam Locke . . . S. C. Adams . . . Ruth Cauthorn . . . Ross Ferris . . . Virginia Botts . . . Loyal Wonneman . . . Willie Beagles . . . Eldon Reed . . . Elsie and Martha Ward . . . Berry Azdell . . . George Adams . . . Maurice Kemp . . . Howard Maxwell . . . Laurene Miller . . . Wallace Witchie . . . Clarence Torreyson . . . Ed Gamble . . . Earl Moore . . . Charles Arnold . . . Margaret Mackie . . . Lakenan Barnes . . . Mary Virginia Melson . . . Alice Fish . . .

The names of many would long be remembered in the community. To some they were reminders of those who shared their high school years—classmates, friends, sweethearts. To others—of a younger age—the names form the record of a generation that learned their lessons well and gave back to their community in many ways the benefits of minds, talents and characters nurtured by this high school.

Hail to thee, McMillan!

33

Blessed with Fire Brick

Over its first half-century the county's settlers cleared woods, opened the prairie and combined progressive methods with hard work and abiding confidence to make Audrain, by the 1880s, one of the state's leading agricultural counties. Through corn and oats, cattle and hogs, mules and horses, farmers were reaping rich benefits. Great wealth lay in Audrain's fertile prairie soil.

Great wealth lay, too, in her exceptional fire clay soil. Fire clay deposits present throughout the county proved to be among the best in the world. Though not as spectacular as striking oil or gold, the discovery and development of fire clay would bring Audrain, after 1910, widespread prosperity.

The importance of fire clay—refractories clay—lay in its capacity to withstand extremely high temperatures without deteriorating or changing form. Brick made from fire clay could be used in making many products that required their containers to undergo severe heat. With increasing success fire brick were used to build industrial furnaces, eventually becoming essential to the production of iron, steel, copper, aluminum, glass, cement and castings. As these basic industries grew, so did the fire brick industry.

Back in the 1840s a few Mexico settlers, like those in many pioneer towns, tried to make use of their clay soil by setting up a pottery. Although such an attempt in Callaway had proved profitable, in Audrain it failed; the clay was somehow ill-suited to earthenware pots and bowls. Even later, in the 1870s and 1880s, renewed efforts to establish a pottery met with glowing promise but little success.

Making bricks for buildings and chimneys met with better luck. By the 1850s bricks made by hand were being used in the construction of a few Mexico houses. After the Civil War the Ketter Brick Works and the A. M. Harrison Brick Yard were producing handmade brick baked in ovens. With little demand and only fair quality, however, such efforts were limited to the small-scale production of building and paving brick.

A few civic leaders sensed that whatever made their soil "different," might also make it valuable. J. A. Glandon, who had moved from Ohio to Mexico in 1875 as the local express agent, was particularly interested in the potential worth of fire clay. Regarded as a young entrepreneur and "live-wire," he had started a telephone exchange, was promoting coal mining on a larger scale—some was already being mined—and was helping to back the elaborate but ill-fated efforts to strike oil in Mexico's Flat Rock area. He also worked with A. M. Harrison in expanding his brick works to make fire brick, but with no marked progress.

Others across the county were becoming interested in fire clay. In search of coal, a Vandalia group in 1883 organized the Audrain Manufacturing and Coal Company; finding more clay than coal, it soon focused on fire brick, but with only limited results. The Mexico Mining and Manufacturing Company was set up in 1886; it shortly became the Salamander Stove Lining and Fire Brick Company, and within months had to again reorganize. The Western Stove Lining Works, established in 1889 by R. E. Elliott, had little initial success but did continue in operation. During these years several such companies were set up, mostly in Mexico, but none did well. Failure followed failure. Among the reasons: a stock market crash, a destructive fire, a railroad strike, an economic depression and a general lack of knowledge about fire brick production.

Still intrigued by stories of the special "white clay" found before the Civil War in southeast Mexico, in 1898 Glandon dug a shaft in this area, finding a large vein of the clay. When bricks made from it were sent to Chicago, tests showed it to be "first class fire brick." More probing revealed that this section of the county contained "unlimited amounts" of fire clay relatively close to the surface—fire clay that would soon be acclaimed as the best in the world.

Determined to produce fire brick, by 1903 Glandon and several Mexico businessmen, including W. W. Fry, J. W. Million, R. M. White, Warren Harper and A. K. Luckie, had obtained enough capital to form the Mexico Brick and Fire Clay Company. Producing building brick as well as fire brick, it operated on a shaky scale through the next six years, gradually eliminating all but fire brick. In 1910 Glandon, in an effort to make some sales, happened to meet with the manager of a St. Louis refractories plant.

In a move that was to deeply affect the future of the county, he wound up selling the entire company to a young engineer named A. P. Green.

Allen Percy Green, from his initial purchase of the struggling little brick company until his death in 1956, became a dominant presence in Mexico and Audrain County. Born in 1875, he spent most of his childhood in Jefferson City and Sedalia. After finishing high school he entered the School of Mines and Metallurgy at Rolla, becoming a civil and mining engineer. Within a few years he became interested in fire brick and accepted a job as manager of a St. Louis company. It was in this capacity that he became aware of the Mexico plant; after trying unsuccessfully to persuade his company to buy it, he decided to buy it himself. The decision meant liquidating his assets and taking great financial risk, a move especially difficult for a young man with a wife and five small children. Nevertheless, in 1910 he moved with his family to Mexico to take over the company.

Convinced of the essential worth of fire brick, he never regretted his decision. He later wrote that at the time he thought that ". . . the quality of Missouri clays, if properly exploited, would result in establishing Missouri as the leading fire brick business in the United States and later of the world. . . . I was convinced also that important developments and improvements were just ahead, which would result in greatly improving the quality and the technique of fire brick manufacture. I believed if I had a free hand I could bring all of this about . . . I was sure of myself and had confidence in my ability to bring these plans into reality."

He was soon introducing big improvements at the small brick plant. Open-pit mining, the elimination of mules in favor of electric power, the tunnel kiln and the dry press manufacturing process were only a few of the changes that would eventually revolutionize the industry. Where others had made little progress, Green excelled. The company benefited from his extensive knowledge and experience in mining, engineering and fire brick production and from his skills in management, promotion and sales. With success apparent and the future assured, in 1915 he was able to incorporate as the A. P. Green Fire Brick Company. By 1937 it had become "the world's largest fireclay plant."

The success of the Fire Brick Company was phenomenal—for Green, for those individuals putting up capital and for those employed, from the furnace stokers to the engineers to the salesmen. It was also a great asset for Mexico and the county, providing jobs, boosting the economy, increasing the flow of dollars across the area and promoting a higher standard of living. All facets of community life were touched by the increasing importance of fire brick: city and county government, railroads, banks, stores, businesses, hospital, real estate, schools, churches and charities. The county basked in its glow.

The fire clay industry was now called "all important" to the county; everyone could see the beauty in pale yellow fire brick. Other fire clay companies were formed. In 1930 the Mexico Refractories Company was organized by J. B. Arthur, who broke away from Green's, establishing his company as a leading competitor. The Western Stove Lining Plant expanded its operations. The Harbison-Walker plant at Vandalia, the Walsh Brothers and North American plants at Farber and others, though smaller, enhanced the significance of the local industry. Audrain County became the acknowledged leader of production in Missouri and the nation. Mexico was hailed as the "Fire Brick Capital of the World."

Advances in the production of fire brick paved the way for other new products and inventions. In Mexico, on the grounds behind Graceland—now his home—Sam P. Locke experimented with a stove that would retain heat overnight and not go out for weeks. His Warm Morning Stove became standard equipment for the military in the coming war as well as a source of comfort for many American homes.

Weathering the Depression years, the local fire brick industry continued to expand and to diversify, playing a major role in World War II, where Green's alone employed more than four thousand workers. As the nation entered the space age a decade or so later, refractories remained an essential industry, adapting to new demands and helping to make possible man's first steps on the moon.

Audrain County now considered its major sources of wealth to be refractories and agriculture. Blessed twofold in her land, her people would continue to develop and to enjoy the manifold benefits of both farm and fire brick.

34

A Hospital for Audrain

During the early years of the twentieth century Audrain county officials and Mexico civic leaders, always eager to improve the community and to promote a better standard of living, were acutely aware of the need for a modern hospital.

Back in 1881 Pinckney French M.D., the first doctor to be born and raised in the county, had established a hospital in a building on the east side of the 400 block of South Jefferson Street, just across the railroad tracks. Although most local doctors supported the project, when he left a few years later to practice in St. Louis, the facility closed. For the next twenty-five years ailing Mexico residents anxious for modern medical care drew little comfort from the fact that the old Globe Hotel down at the corner of Liberty and Water Streets housed "the largest horse infirmary in the State." There was no such refuge for people.

Frequently mentioned as one of the community's primary needs, the general hospital idea finally took hold and became a reality. Some said it owed its start to a bet and a dare.

On a spring evening in 1912 two friends and civic leaders, A. P. Green, of the rising Fire Brick Company, and Colonel Robert M. White, editor of the *Mexico Ledger,* were walking up South Jefferson Street to a city council meeting. Arriving early, they sat down on the high curb beside City Hall to continue their discussion of the town's problems. Green soon brought up the matter of a hospital, and White responded with a challenge.

For months, said the Colonel, Green had been complaining about the town's lack of a hospital. He had bemoaned the fact that the railroad hospital at Moberly—the only one outside of St. Louis and Kansas City—was no place to send an injured brick worker. He had often wished for a hospital in Mexico. It was time, said White, to stop talking and start doing.

Green at once said he was ready to put up money—if the colonel would match it. And, reported a witness, he wrote out a check and handed it to White, who quickly wrote out his own. Green later said they each contributed "about $2,500."

It was enough to start a fund for a hospital. The Mexico Commercial Club backed the project. City and county officials were in favor. Doctors contributed. Business leaders approved and promised assistance. Individuals pledged support, and so, eventually, did people across the entire county—support both financial and moral.

Backers then organized the Mexico Hospital Association. Their goal became a community hospital with facilities for general surgery and modern medical care. While Green, as president, visited institutions across the nation, gathering information about organization and management, other officers sought financial backing, collecting nearly $20,000 in cash.

The former Windsor Hotel, at the southeast corner of Jackson and Clark, was selected as the best available site. Rented at $50 a month, the three-story building was to be repaired, cleaned, papered, painted and disinfected in a "most thorough manner." Its interior would then be outfitted with the best medical equipment their funds could buy.

The whole town pitched in to help. The *Ledger* strongly supported it, reminding readers that "You said you wanted a hospital, you promised to assist . . . come on in and make a cash contribution." People from all sections of the community responded. Businesses, church groups, fraternal orders, civic clubs, charitable organizations and women's societies gave time and energy as well as dollars. Storeowners contributed wallpaper, a three-burner gas stove, knives and forks, a half-dozen pillows, a sewing machine and an "operating table." Gifts from the public at a Saturday afternoon Hospital Shower included an ice chest, a teakettle, dustpans, pie pans, a clothes hamper, a two-quart percolator and an eggbeater.

Several hospital benefits, with performers entertaining in homes, were held, bringing in a few dollars. The Darnaby Company, northeast Missouri's producer of plays, offered 25 percent of the gate from its new musical, *The Flirt*. Ladies in its cast formed "The Beauty Chorus Boosters" and canvassed the town for donations; their performance on stage was wildly cheered, assuring the success of the show—and of the hospital. *The Flirt* produced an impressive one hundred dollars for the fund.

In December the Board opened the new hospital with an evening dedication ceremony that drew a large and admiring crowd. Mexico Mayor Willard Potts and County Judge Alex Carter made speeches, the Presbyterian pastor offered a prayer and the Baptist Quartet sang. Mr. Green presided over the program, introducing dignitaries and making brief remarks. He was, he said, honored to be "tendering the use of the hospital to the city of Mexico and Audrain County."

After the program visitors were encouraged to tour the building and stop by the x-ray room. There, with this new invention they could "inspect the inner framework of their hand" and enjoy the "unique sensation of looking through the hand and seeing the bones." Punch and cake were served in the basement, and thirty-six dollars added to the fund.

At first the twenty-bed facility averaged only three or four patients, usually accident victims. Gradually more took advantage of its services, with doctors performing surgery in its operating room and referring the sick to its care. It was six months before it welcomed its first baby; to promote its use mothers of baby boys were presented with a dozen red roses, mothers of girls, with yellow. When a train wreck near Centralia brought in eighty injured passengers for emergency treatment, the hospital's importance was acknowledged by everyone in the community.

Proud as they were of their achievement, the board was soon investigating ways to expand and improve the hospital. Green in particular felt that the people of Mexico and Audrain were entitled to medical care and facilities as good as any in the nation, insisting that they needed a modern new building and better sources of funding. He took the lead in urging the Missouri legislature and the Governor to pass the 1917 County Hospital Law. This allowed a special tax and the issuing of bonds for county hospitals, a growing trend across the nation.

Audrain was the first to take advantage of the new law, in 1918 establishing Missouri's first county hospital. The original bond issue of $75,000 passed easily. When World War I and the necessity for a Supreme Court ruling to uphold the new law brought delay and higher construction costs, county residents passed a second bond issue for an additional $40,000. Voters in effect were doubly approving their hospital, reinforcing its role in the county.

In December 1920, the first Mexico Hospital was closed, its assets having been smoothly transferred to the elected Board of Directors of the new Audrain Hospital. In appreciation of his faithful support and dedication during its difficult early years, the Board honored Mr. Green with the title Father of the Audrain Hospital. He and his wife would continue their generosity to this realization of his vision.

The new hospital was built on East Monroe Street, on the south side of the 600 block. At the groundbreaking ceremony the guest speaker offered congratulations "upon this auspicious beginning of a splendid work." It was his hope, he said, that it would be "an increasing and ever continuing source of comfort, satisfaction and relief."

And this it has, indeed, proved to be.

35

Any Mail Today?

T he arrival of the first posted mail bearing the address *Mexico, Audrain County, Missouri* caused a stir of excitement in that small prairie village. John Bingle Morris, appointed the first postmaster in 1837, received the first mail and operated the first post office at his Green Tree Tavern for the next fifteen years. One or two days a week most of the village gathered to hear him "cry out the mail." He would hand over what was claimed by those present and, until he happened to see someone due a letter, carry the rest around in the brim of his tall black hat.

In the county's early days mail was sent by riverboat from St. Louis to Louisiana, Hannibal or Jefferson City, and then by courier on horseback to Mexico; later it arrived by stagecoach. Postage, figured by the distance a letter traveled and considered costly, was paid by the person receiving it. For years mail arriving at the Tavern—usually a few letters and perhaps a newspaper or two—was light in volume, since many families received nothing and others only three or four letters a year. Postmaster Morris got to know everyone in the county and, since he probably accommodated those who could not read, much of their personal business.

Most correspondence, particularly that from "back home" in Kentucky or Virginia, reported news of great importance such as a family death, someone's failing health, or an impending trip to Missouri by prospective settlers or an adventurous relative. Letters were often weeks or even months in reaching their destination, and then might languish at the post office until the addressee happened to ride into town and thought to check for mail.

In the years before the Civil War other post offices were established in the county, some to quickly close. Among the earliest were Salt River, Shy Post, Hickory Creek or Barneyville, Littleby or Progress, Omelet, John's Branch, Young's Creek and Loutre. As railroads were built, offices opened along their right-of-way, making mail delivery easier and quicker. As the population increased, so did the mail.

In Mexico, as other postmasters succeeded Morris, the post office was located wherever it was most convenient. The *1876 City Directory* lists it at the "2d d n of nw cor Square"—the second door north of the northwest corner of the Square—in what would become known as the Ledger Building. Here it remained for around ten years.

It was about this time that Postmaster George Poteet wrote to Washington saying that he badly needed a clerk. New mail routes from St. Louis and Kansas City now made a total of seven mails received and seven dispatched daily from town by railroad, plus four by horse and buggy. Whether he got the requested help is not known, but a successor soon afterward was enjoying a paid assistant in the form of his son, Luther Saunders. Luther, age ten, stood on a box to sort the mail, quit school to perform his duties and remained with the post office for the next forty-one years.

During the 1890s, federal regulations required that the post office be open from 3 to 4 o'clock on Sundays and appointed holidays, and on all other days from 7 A.M. to 7 P.M. The cost of mailing "letters or other matter sealed" was 2c per ounce. Newspapers, third-class circulars and other matter cost 1c. "Liquids, Flour, Salves, Medicines, etc.," stated the regulations, were "unmailable except under certain conditions and will be excluded from the mails as soon as their character is discovered." Money orders could be purchased at 5c for sums under $5, graduating to 45c for $100.

Residents usually called at the post office once a day to pick up the mail. If something special was expected they might make a second trip when the afternoon trains came through. While some rented a box and could collect their own, many stopped at the counter to ask, "Any mail today?"

By 1892 the Mexico office had moved to the northwest corner of Jefferson and Promenade, where it shared a building with a variety store. When W. M. Treloar was named postmaster in 1898, he moved it to the southwest corner of Promenade and Washington, into a new building distinguished by a green marble column at the corner entrance.

In 1913 Congressman Champ Clark acquired an appropriation for Mexico's first "Federal Building," and for the next fifty-four years mail was handled at this impressive granite and limestone structure at Jackson and Clark. Postmasters who served here included Rufus Jackson, L. M.

Gamble, Mrs. W. C. Stewart (for a record tenure of eighteen years), Miss Margaret Mackie and—the last appointed through the old political system—R. C. Romdall, who would retire in 1973 from another new post office farther down West Jackson.

Mexico residents began receiving their mail at home during the 1890s, with deliveries for a while made twice a day. In 1901 carriers were delivering mail by horse and postal buggy to farmers out in the county through a new program known as Rural Free Delivery. Mexico began with two routes, soon expanded to four; Vandalia with one.

By the 1920s thirty-four post offices had opened at one time or another across the county. As automobiles and better roads became more common, deliveries were consolidated to provide better service. Offices began to combine, by 1958 giving the county only eight: Mexico, Farber, Martinsburg, Rush Hill, Laddonia, Vandalia, Thompson and Benton City.

Parcel post, V-Mail, air mail, zip codes and stamps, rising from 2c in 1920, to 3c from 1932 through the mid-1950s, to 10c in 1974, were some of the changes introduced to the letter-writing public over the years.

Despite the spread of telephones and other signs of progress, the mail would remain a familiar and necessary part of everyday life: postcards and bills, tax forms and Sears & Roebuck catalogs, invitations and advertisements, Christmas greetings and birthday cards, letters from grandmothers and letters from boyfriends. And, in many an outgoing mail, letters from home.

VIII

The Best Community in the Entire Middle West

36

The Protracted Picnic

In the early 1900s, as dust, humidity and searing summer heat began to tax mind, body and spirit, many Mexico and Audrain residents, seeking cool shade and good company, moral uplift and fun for all, escaped their daily routine and headed for the Chautauqua.

The Mexico Chautauqua Assembly was established in 1906 as a part of the national movement that for nearly fifty years offered summer programs of secular education, religious instruction and wholesome entertainment in an outdoor setting. Described as a mixture of revival meeting and county fair, the movement began in 1873 at a Methodist camp meeting in the New York town of Chautauqua. It soon crossed church boundaries and expanded to attract many followers, at its peak around 1915 sponsoring some twenty-two thousand meetings across the United States and Canada.

The Mexico group, under the leadership of Sam Locke, R. D. Worrell, Hardin College president J. W. Million and others, was pleased to receive "hearty endorsement" for their initial efforts in 1906. Promising "rest and recreation for the body," along with "social and intellectual stimulus" and "entertainment for the mind," they carefully planned the second annual program of July 16–25, 1907—a "protracted picnic of ten days."

The camp was set up at "Wade Grove," a 75-acre tract in northwest Mexico. In walking distance of downtown, it provided ample room for the assembly's tents, one of which could seat three thousand. It also had plenty of good water, could be easily lighted at night and with its groves of trees of good water, could be easily lighted at night and with its groves of trees offered shady areas for study meetings and family gatherings.

Tickets for the entire Chautauqua sold at $2 for adults and $1 for children six to twelve; children under six were admitted free. Admission for one day began at 35c, with the warning that one could not return once departing the grounds. Tents could be rented for $3.50 and up, cots for $1, camp chairs for 25c and stools for 20c.

Everyone was encouraged to eat in the dining hall tent or at the refreshment stand; prices were moderate. The management provided free ice water, special police to ensure order, a bureau of information and the ringing of bells to mark the time. They also set up a headquarters tent where all local churches could be represented. No selling of goods or soliciting for trade were allowed.

The formal program began at nine o'clock each morning. Small children went to kindergarten, boys and girls aged six to sixteen to the Seton Indian Club and their mothers and other ladies to the "physical culture" class for "improving the health and acquiring ease and grace of movement." An elocution class, set for 10 A.M., issued an invitation to "everyone who wants to read well and to understand good literature." The Woman's Christian Temperance Union scheduled meetings, as did the Chautauqua Round Table, a discussion group, with other events at hourly intervals.

Recreation facilities included swings, lawn tennis, baseball and croquet. On one afternoon a spelling match was held, with captains choosing sides and a director selecting words from the old blueback speller; anyone over sixteen could compete for the $10 prize. Interspersed through the day's program were performances by soloists and such musical groups as the Lyric Glee Club and the Lakeside Quartette of Chicago. By eight o'clock a growing crowd anticipated the highlight of each evening, a spellbinding speaker on a subject well chosen to touch the heartstrings of the audience.

Gradually the movement became more commercial, offering programs of more popular appeal. The Mexico Banner Program of 1913 promoted a "splendid company" of grand opera stars, the Spanish Ladies' Orchestra and "Thaviu and His Band of Forty." It also featured lecturer Judge A. Z. Blair, "a terror to evil-doers," and Ralph Parlette, speaking on the University of Hard Knocks.

A great favorite of most audiences was Edwin R. Weeks, "genius" and "merry man," who impersonated Presidents Taft, Teddy Roosevelt and Woodrow Wilson, and also the pianist Paderewski. Mirth and music were blended in this event, stated the brochure, and everyone was urged to "laugh and grow fat."

30, 1913, included a talk on the "Land of the Dragon" (China) by one who had been there, a male quartet and bell ringers, and Shungopavi, the "Great Indian Mystery Man." A star performance was given by Mary Agnes Doyle, lecturer and elocutionist—"when you have heard her your brain will be clearer and your heart lighter. She is good for the blues and has lifted tons of grief from human lives."

This brochure also printed *A Chautauqua Psalm*. Among its verses:

The chautauqua comes but once a year. It affords opportunities I shall surely grasp while they are here . . .

I am not selfish. So I shall take my folks with me of course . . .

I want my wife to get the thrill of it all. My boy shall hear the great speeches. My girl will like the music.

The commonplace experiences of every day incline one to become hidebound and also cultivate ingrowing dispositions.

The chautauqua shakes us up and shakes us loose. I want to be so shaken. Shake with me . . . It is my chautauqua. Nobody can enjoy it for me. I shall take pleasure in doing all the enjoying I can, up to my capacity . . .

From all over the surrounding countryside people came to the Mexico Chautauqua. They were shaken. And they enjoyed.

37

Riding Audrain's Trolley

C*lang, clang, clang went the trolley* . . . not only along the streets of St. Louis, but also across the cornfields of Audrain County. For a half-dozen years the Mexico, Santa Fe and Perry Traction Company served a portion of the county with its "electric line" and trolley cars.

Mexico residents were already familiar with trolleys, run not by electricity but by horsepower. In 1889 the town had, in the spirit of progress, granted a franchise for a city streetcar line. Tracks were laid out South Clark Street and west along the dusty Hardin College Boulevard to the Fair Grounds at the southwest city limits. Three cars traveled the line, each drawn by a team of horses.

While at first residents eagerly backed this modern effort at easier transportation, their enthusiasm soon waned. Passengers often had to get off to lighten the load so the horses could pull the car across a slope or around a corner, and sometimes were asked to help set the car back in place when it jumped the track—a frequent occurrence. The venture soon folded, one newspaper noting that "after one ride the public refused to court death or injury in a similar manner again."

Twenty years later local businessmen organizing the Mexico, Santa Fe and Perry Traction Company—commonly known as the MSF & PT—were more optimistic about trolleys powered by electricity. In 1909 they obtained a streetcar franchise from the city council for a line running north from Mexico to Santa Fe, in Monroe County, for both passengers and freight.

On the afternoon of March 1, 1910, a crowd gathered near Western and Love Streets for special ceremonies initiating construction of the trolley tracks for the new company. It was an auspicious occasion marked by officials "driving the golden spike" into the new track. In the minds of many, ever optimistic, the undertaking signaled a new era of progress for the county and city, now destined to become the center of a great "interurban system" of transportation.

During its first year the company built a powerhouse near Davis Fork, its source of electricity, and completed the first mile of track. By 1911 a nine-mile stretch to Molino was done, and by 1915 passengers were traveling the additional seven miles to Santa Fe. From there construction never continued, for original plans to connect at Perry with a railroad to Hannibal were never realized, nor was an extension of the line from Mexico south toward Fulton.

Two passenger cars were operated by the line, one yellow and the other gray. Each boasted rows of comfortable seats, windows for ventilation and a powerful spotlight at the head of the car for illuminating the path after dark. At least one freight car was in use for transporting cattle and grain. Power was provided through a long arm reaching from the top of a car to the electric cable strung above the length of the track. To turn around, the conductor simply reversed the arm and took off in the opposite direction.

Tickets on the "Mexico Railroad" sold for five cents. A passenger bought as many tickets as were needed to reach his destination, a one-way trip to Santa Fe costing forty-five cents. Speed was not of utmost importance; schedules were haphazard at best. Bad weather caused delays, as did problems with the power supply, difficulty in loading cattle on the freight car and cows lying on the track.

A variety of customers enjoyed the trolley. Farm families welcomed it for business and shopping trips into Mexico. Town residents delighted in riding up to Molino or Santa Fe to spend the day with friends or relatives living near the line. A number of McMillan High School students rode the cars daily, often arriving late at the Western Avenue Station and consequently facing afternoon detention hall for tardiness. Groups planning picnics, all-day excursions and family outings especially liked the trolley, for it offered an inexpensive and safe ride to several desirable sites. On some occasions, such as the evening ice-cream socials held at the Sunrise Christian Church, the streetcar also provided power for lighting the churchyard.

In spite of its early success the MSF & PT Company lasted only a few years. It gradually became apparent that the rural population it served could not adequately support it. Improvements in county roads and the growing importance of the automobile also contributed to its decline. By 1919 the electric line had yielded to still more modern ways and Audrain residents had ridden their last trolley.

38

Mexico Calling!

There was a time when a Mexico resident wishing to "reach out and touch someone" cranked the handle of his wall telephone and rang up Central. The voice of the Mexico Telephone Company, Central supplied a vast array of facts and services: the correct time at any hour of the day or night; the arrival and departure times of trains, and those running late; moving picture shows currently playing; baseball and football schedules and the scores of any games. If you had an emergency, Central summoned the Fire Department or located your doctor. If you needed to be awakened at a certain time, Central would oblige. If you were going out of town, Central would gladly pass on to those calling you any messages as to where you were, when you would return and where to send your mail. And if, of course, you simply wanted to place a call, she would ring your party—no number necessary.

Mexico was introduced to the telephone in 1884 by J. A. Glandon, the local express agent and main force behind setting up a telephone company. As early as 1881 the *Ledger* was reporting that over a hundred poles had been erected and "most of the wire strung" for an anticipated seventy-five instruments. Since only twenty customers—city hall, a few stores, the two railroad offices, the Windsor Hotel, a couple of attorneys, two banks and a livery stable—actually subscribed to the service, limiting its usefulness, the venture was short-lived and out of commission by the following year.

The next company was established in 1892 by E. D. Graham and his two sons, Charles and Gus, who "built, owned and operated" the exchange.

Opening with forty-eight subscribers, in two years the business had expanded to one hundred and sixty. In 1901 the Grahams sold the business, the exchange becoming the Mexico Telephone Company.

The Telephone Company occupied two offices in the city. The business office and the exchange handling local calls were located on the second floor of the Steinman Shoe Store on South Washington Street, while the long distance apparatus filled an office over the First National Bank on South Jefferson.

Under the direction of the president, a manager, one lineman and a "trouble shooter," the company grew rapidly, expanding its services. The first rural area to be served was Benton City, with other towns soon joining for a total of seven hundred and fifty phones by 1907.

Customers were billed quarterly at $27 a year for a business desk phone and $18 a year for a one-party residence wall set. Customers could also subscribe to party line service, sharing the line with as many as three other parties. Local calls were free, with charges of 25c for five minutes within a twenty-five mile radius of Mexico. Listing local and long distance connections, a *Subscribers' Directory* was distributed, with patrons requested to call by number and "when through talking ring off."

Six operators sat on tall chairs in front of a bank of plugs, wires and handles to manage the telephone system. Although at first operated only by men, young women soon proved preferable. Required to wear white blouses and black skirts in summer and all black in winter in order to present a "business-like" appearance, they worked long shifts at salaries averaging two dollars a week. Assets for the job were a pleasant voice, a tenacious memory and the capacity to refrain from tattling—curiosity, however, and a knack for listening in were not necessarily prohibited.

In 1911 the company was absorbed by the Bell System, its name changing to the Missouri and Kansas Telephone Company. All equipment was moved into a new building at the northeast corner of Promenade and Coal Streets. Salaries rose to $15 a month for six nine-hour days a week, increasing to $18 after three months on the job. Operators also worked ten-hour Sundays twice a month.

Over the next twenty years the Mexico exchange expanded to more than two thousand telephones. The large wall crank-box with its separate mouthpiece and hearing cone in due course gave way to the heavy black dial model, and eventually, after another twenty years, to the colored plastic push-button.

By the 1950s, with the system a part of Southwestern Bell Telephone, every store and business and most homes would install at least one phone, if not several. After first memorizing two digits for their phone number, such as 44, residents soon added two more numbers and a word, making it, for example, JUstice 2211. They then prefaced each listing with 581. Finally they attached the 314 area code (still later to change to 573) to complete their telephone number.

A century and more after the telephone's first ring echoed through Mexico the friendly voice of Central is no longer available. But the telephone has become an essential part of life and remains a favorite way to reach out and touch the world.

39

Dark Days, Trying Times

During the 1930s—after the 1929 stock market crash and through much of the following decade—the county and the country were mired in what history would call the depths of the Depression. Financial failure and economic distress spread across America. Times were hard and money in short supply. In the face of grim reality, people viewed the future with pessimism and only cautious, wistful hope. The nation's economy, prospects and morale were at a rock-bottom low.

Circumstances defining the Depression for the rest of the nation were true as well for Audrain County. Banks failed. In Mexico the Southern, the Farmers and Merchants and the North Missouri Trust "went under." Savings disappeared. Money was scarce. Although the county's leading industries continued in operation and the area fared better than some, cuts were made. Production went down. Sales diminished.

Jobs vanished. Many businesses closed, while others barely managed to stay open. Some employees took lower pay, others were let go. Those seeking jobs could find no work—not even at the corner garage or "filling station." There was money only for the necessities of life. Good, hardworking people went broke. Unable to pay bills or taxes, many took bankruptcy. One Mexico college graduate postponed his own life to spend the next dozen years paying off his family's debts; it was, he said, a matter of honor.

Farmers in this strong agricultural area suffered from low market prices and failed crops. By the mid-1930s Audrain listed 4,900 delinquent taxpayers; many, though not all, were farmers. The county ranked third in the state for foreclosures. All felt the sadness as farms, some for generations in the same family, passed into the hands of insurance companies or were sold at the steps of the Court House.

The Depression affected everyone in one way or another. Some faced dire poverty. Others "tightened their belts" and plodded on. Some had no food, others no heat, a few no home. One former city official was found living in little better than a paper shack. For a job, one man ran a popcorn stand at the corner of the Square.

Public relief soared. Considered by many a disgrace, such aid was given to more and more families by Mexico's Social Service Association. By the end of 1933 the county was contributing a substantial $250 a month as its share in caring for the city's needy. During one winter $5,000 was asked of industries, businesses, individuals and civic clubs to bolster the local relief fund. At the Depression's lowest point over two hundred Audrain families were on welfare, a heavy load; in one year nearly 2,400 individuals received aid. Miss Cora Darrah, the social service nurse, worked through the schools to provide children with used clothing, shoes, haircuts, medical and dental care. Churches took care of many, trying to meet difficult demands with limited resources.

Reminders of hard times were everywhere. Despite valiant efforts, Hardin College stood empty. Missouri Military Academy, saved from a similar fate by its reorganization, lowered fees and in one case accepted an Oriental rug for a cadet's tuition. Public school teachers were paid lower salaries, used worn, outdated textbooks and forgot about new supplies. Audrain Hospital nurses worked longer hours for less pay. Hoboes riding the railroad knocked at back doors, offering to work for food. Houses went unpainted, repairs unmade. Clothes were patched, mended, made over and handed down. People "made do" with what they had.

Even the weather matched the pattern of misery. Dust storms blew in, resting their "dark pall" over Audrain and filling the air with grit. Unpredictable extremes brought several summers of "prevailing drouth," with one year in between so wet farmers could not plant crops. The heat reached all-time highs. Mexico set a record of 116 degrees in July of 1934; 1936 saw 49 days with temperatures at 100 or above. In these years of few refrigerators and little air conditioning, the Power Company produced 60,000 tons of ice each day and imported 25,000 more, at times limiting each household to a daily 25 pounds. Only the Jefferson Hotel and the Liberty Theater had "air cooling." To survive the heat people slept at night in basements, on front porches and in backyards.

Reflecting the optimism inspired by President Franklin Roosevelt—

whom Audrain helped elect in 1932 by a vote of 7,301 to 2,037—the county welcomed federal agencies and public works projects. New offices were opened for them at the Court House. Public officials urged the public to support their efforts to get the country "back on course." Ministers in particular complied, praising from the pulpit these attempts to fight Depression evils of "bigotry, greed, and indifference."

Initially providing 250 jobs at 30c an hour for 15 hours a week, these federal work projects included the extension of sewer and water lines, improvements at Garfield School and Mexico High School, the painting of buildings, the graveling of county roads and the paving of the Square. Even the Court House was redecorated "inside and out," its exterior acquiring the new look that marked its latter years, and its clock a facelift with new Arabic numerals.

The Agricultural Adjustment Administration, spending a quarter million dollars locally, aided farmers by granting subsidies and controlling production. In July, 1936, County Agent Glen Mutti wired the U.S. secretary of agriculture: "Pastures burned up. No feed. Corn suffering . . . relief needed, Audrain County, Mo." In a few weeks over a hundred additional jobs were set up for county farmers at $34.56 a month. About the same time the Civilian Conservation Corps accepted a local quota of around thirty young men in their camps; wages were sent home to parents.

Life went on. After 1934 the local economy showed some signs of improvement. The Shoe Factory added workers, up by 100 to 615. Several employers, Green's and Mexico Refractories leading the way, cooperated with federal guidelines for a 40-hour week and a 40c-an-hour minimum wage.

There were other signs of recovery. The Savings Bank moved into its new brick building on the old Ringo lot; its former home, diagonally across on Jefferson, became Woolworth's Five and Dime. Pilcher's and the Hotel Hoxsey put up "big city" electric signs. Mexico Refractories moved its offices into the former Elks Building at Love and Coal. With more people ready to spend a nickel for an ice-cold Coca-Cola in its chunky green bottle, the bottling works moved into its new building on North Jefferson Street. The new city police car arrived—a Chevrolet.

Life was not without its pleasures. Many people enjoyed a good "movin' picture show." At the Liberty or the Rex adults paid a quarter and children a dime to see Will Rogers, Shirley Temple, Clark Gable, Joan Crawford, Fred Astaire, Ginger Rogers and a host of other stars. "Funny papers" drew smiles; *The Katzenjammer Kids, Little Orphan Annie, Buck Rogers, Maggie and Jiggs, Dick Tracy* and *Flash Gordon* were favorites.

Radio, now ensconced in most living rooms, was fascinating—and free. Listeners tuned in H. V. Kaltenborn, Kate Smith, Jack Benny, Burns and Allen, boxing matches and baseball games, *One Man's Family, Charlie McCarthy, Your Hit Parade* and, on every week night, *Amos 'n' Andy*. Mexico's own Willie Morris—one of Judge Morris's great-grandchildren—made good in New York; everyone dialed NBC-Blue for her familiar lyric soprano. On Monday nights, over KSD–St. Louis, friends and fans listened to Jane Rodgers, another native daughter, "singing the news of the day in clever rhymes..."

The Kiwanis Club, with help from friends, staged an annual Minstrel Show, presenting the town with extra relief funds, a hilarious evening and stars of its own. Housewives looked forward to the *Ledger*'s annual three-day Cooking School. Everybody checked on Mexico's marathon skater, Asa Hall, as he roller-skated across the nation.

Ladies spent the day in St. Louis, catching the early morning train, shopping and lunching at Stix, and returning in the evening. Baseball fans motored down to see the Browns or Cardinals play. Young and old stayed home to work jigsaw and crossword puzzles and to play bridge and the new financial game called Monopoly.

The Depression left its mark on this entire generation. People knew hard times, but felt also a spirit of concern and cooperation. Many would recall an obligation to look after their own. Most experienced a willingness to pull together and a determination to unite, as families and as a community, to face whatever might come. In spite of the hardships and difficulties, these years reflected credit upon many.

In 1936, when Audrain celebrated its one-hundreth birthday, Mexico Mayor Gus Graham, in a Centennial Proclamation, praised the way her people, with their "right psychology" and "determined efforts," had weathered the recent "period of reverses." Their history showed, he said, "that every period of distress has been met and conquered just as the city and county have done throughout the last five years . . ."

The Depression years were not yet over, and happy days not yet come again. But gray skies were clearing, and there was cause to look for a rainbow.

40

Viva, Audrain! Mexico, Olé!

I n August of 1936 Mexico and Audrain County enjoyed a week-long celebration of the one-hundredth anniversary of their founding. Old settlers were remembered, their first century praised and a new one of anticipated progress hailed.

Planning had begun months earlier with the appointment of centennial city and county commissions to organize the gala celebration. In recognition of the origin of their name, officials from "Old Mexico" were invited to attend, and in a gesture of confidence in the future, substantial sums were spent to revive the Audrain County Fair. Congratulations were in order. *Viva, Audrain! Mexico, Olé!*

It was a week eagerly anticipated. On the first day dignitaries arriving in town were escorted by special motorcycle police out to the Fair Grounds, where the celebration was formally opened with speeches and a carefully timed salvo of guns. The official delegation from the Republic of Mexico, led by Señor Manuel Cruz G., was honored at an impressive ceremony where an exchange of gifts brought the City of Mexico a trophy, a scroll and the silver sombrero that became the symbol of the Centennial Fiesta Fair.

In a welcoming speech the Honorable Clarence Cannon, the district's representative to Congress, greeted visitors and congratulated the county upon its historic milestone. He also formally announced, as the center of the celebration, the return of the Audrain County Fair. The Fair Committee was to be greatly commended, he said, for resuming, after a lapse of twenty years, this "happy custom."

Festivities galore filled the week: livestock and horse shows, military and aerial exhibitions, a fireworks display, a Parade of Bands, a Religious Day on Sunday with basket dinners and a speaking, an Old Fiddlers Contest, a Fire Clay Day and an open-air gala dance. Saddle horses paced the famed track as of old, ribbons and prizes were awarded once more and a queen and her court again ruled in splendor—Miss Darlene Nichols received the most votes among fifty-one young ladies vying for the honor.

Signs with a Mexican motif dotted the Square. Stores offered specials with a Mexican touch. Local señoritas donned tasseled skirts and shawls and the Fair Grounds, dazzling in new grandeur, were filled with supporters wearing bright straw sombreros. Except for a proposed bullfight—which met with skepticism—everything Mexican was cheered.

The main parade, featuring several bands and over forty floats, stretched for a mile along West Boulevard past thousands of spectators. Honored dignitaries included, besides the Mexican delegation and Representative Cannon, Missouri Governor Guy Park, U.S. Senators Bennett Clark and Harry Truman, state senator Frank Hollingsworth, county officials and the centennial chairman, B. Turner Williams.

The highlight of the week was the Centennial Pageant, a musical extravaganza named *Mexicali.* An estimated twenty thousand people, on three evenings, attended the show. Through story, song and scenery hundreds of volunteers depicted the founding and growth of Mexico and Audrain County.

For most residents the Centennial was a time for saluting early settlers, praising city fathers and relishing their collective accomplishments. Old-timers recalled stories of the county's early days. Mrs. Malinda Mansfield French, who as a little girl had watched her father lay out the village of Mexico, was congratulated at her home in St. Louis for reaching her 104th birthday. The *Mexico Evening Ledger* published a commemorative Centennial Edition devoted to the county's history, individuals responsible for its progress, and its status at this significant anniversary.

In a Centennial Proclamation Mexico Mayor Gus Graham voiced his pride in Mexico and Audrain for their development into "one of the most important commercial and marketing centers" in the state. To fully appreciate their remarkable prosperity and steadfast growth, he said, it was important to review some of their civic "possessions."

Many of these assets and points of civic pride the *Ledger* printed as a long list of facts "with which Every Audrain County Citizen Should Be

Familiar." The county's population stood at 22,000; that of Mexico at 8,721. In this centennial year they were "the center of the saddle horse world" and "the center of the fireclay industry of the nation." Audrain County led the state in production of oats and soybeans, and ranked among its leaders for wheat, corn, wool and poultry. It also bred "many fine herds of blooded cattle and swine, to say nothing of the saddle horses being raised here."

Listed as major industries were the A. P. Green Fire Brick, Mexico Refractories, Western Stove Lining, International Shoe, Continental Banking Supply and Continental Bag Companies. Two of the nation's largest chicken hatcheries were in Mexico, plus the Pollock flour mill (home of "Daisy, the Flour of the Family"), a grain elevator, two bottling plants, an extensive greenhouse, a modern laundry and "an ice cream and butter factory." While many local firms bore "favorable known family names," said the *Ledger,* there were also many "newer firms and faces," all ready to lead the county into a successful second century.

Governed by a mayor and a council of four, the county seat was a city known for its stability. Mexico employed a chief of police and five policemen, a fire chief and driver and a fire plugman for its "motorized Fire Department," a cemetery sexton, a street commissioner and an operator for its $100,000 septic tank. Its citizens were served by a $100,000 post office, an "up-to-date" telephone company and a utility company that supplied electricity, water, ice, gas and heat. Its new airport was a major asset, as were its two railroad lines, thirty-two daily buses, and its location on state routes 22 and 15 and "Federal Highway No. 54." They benefited also from twenty miles of brick-paved streets and "many other hard surfaced and oiled residence streets."

Residents derived great satisfaction from their modern $150,000 Audrain Hospital, currently planning an addition, and from their extensive public library. They enjoyed three modern hotels, three auditoriums—"with a total seating capacity of 3,000"—and two theaters, one with air-conditioning. They supported two newspapers—the *Mexico Intelligencer* and the *Mexico Evening Ledger.* A Rotary and a Kiwanis Club drew community conscious members, and a "live Mexico Civic Club with a paid secretary" promoted the city.

Educational establishments included two private schools, St. Brendan's Parochial and Missouri Military Academy. Four public schools were in operation: McMillan, Garfield, South Side, soon to be replaced by the new Eugene Field School, and the $300,000 Mexico High School. Nine churches had active congregations: the Methodist, Baptist, Christian, Catholic, Presbyterian, Episcopalian, Christian Science, Holiness and Lutheran.

As to recreational facilities, a municipal athletic field was in use, along with a supervised public playground (in Hardin Park), a "public bathing beach with safety guards" (Kiwanis Lake behind the high school) and two "modern natatoriums." Two tourist parks catered to vacationers motoring through town.

Waving sombreros in salute, Audrain and Mexico residents enthusiastically celebrated a past of which they could be "justly prideful." With high hopes for their second century, they congratulated themselves upon being, as Mayor Graham put it, "in the class of one of the best communities in the entire middle west."

In the spirit of 1936, *Viva, Audrain! Mexico, Olé!*

IX

With Indomitable
Spirit

41

School: The Common Bond

School days in an endless string bind together the children of a generation—the shared experience of going to school in the same span of time. School days in a chain unbroken link one generation to those past and future—the shared experience of going to school in the same place. This, in turn, shapes the history of a community.

By the 1970s the people of Audrain were completing a century of progress in providing public education for their children. The long slow process had been discouraging at times and often demanding in terms of financial support and dedication. But it had consistently moved forward, reflecting the determination of parents and the vision and commitment of school boards across the county.

For several decades, high schools in the larger towns, along with better roads and school buses, had made a public high school education possible for all children in the county. Now across the state plans were made for the transportation of more and more elementary as well as secondary pupils to larger, more centrally located schools. Small rural districts—some of which, for various reasons, had already closed over the years—were now all to disband. Parents of rural students demanded better and more modern facilities; this was financially feasible only with the consolidation of districts.

One by one the country schools closed. Some combined into larger districts: Community R-VI, with Martinsburg, Laddonia, Rush Hill, Benton City and twenty-two rural districts, was set up in 1949 and Highway R-III, still later to be absorbed by Mexico, in 1951. Vandalia and Farber joined into the Van-Far District in 1956. Others merged into the Mexico District. The first to be annexed into Mexico, in 1950, was Lawder; the last to close, in 1973, was Carter.

As a result of these closings, with a large portion of the county now sending children into the Mexico system, its educational jurisdiction was extended and its tax base expanded. The enrollment soared. Many parents, wanting the best possible schools, also indicated a willingness to provide financial support. Always the goal was better education, a system of excellence.

Part of the story of this continuing educational progress over the years can be seen in a review of Mexico's school buildings. In 1908, when McMillan High School opened, there were three other public schools in town. The oldest, the original Public School of 1873, across North Olive Street from the Christian Church, had been known for some time as North Side. Garfield School, located at the end of East Breckenridge, had opened in the early 1890s, serving black children in town; the bond issue that built McMillan allowed also for Garfield's second, larger building. Another elementary school called South Side had been built in 1895 in the 800 block of West Breckenridge for children living south of the railroad tracks.

Over the next six decades—from 1912 into the 1970s—the Mexico Board of Education faced an almost constant demand for more classrooms. Besides an increasing number of rural high school students, the population was consistently growing, bringing a natural increase in school enrollment. Truancy laws, requiring school attendance between the ages of eight and sixteen, were more rigidly enforced. Students began to stay in school longer, with a higher percentage graduating from high school.

By 1920 Superintendent L. B. Hawthorne was suggesting "a wonderful new high school for the future." This would ease the district's overcrowding and meet higher standards now required by the state. Five years later a bond issue for $300,000 was proposed for a new high school to be built on an eighty-eight-acre site in the city's northwest area. In spite of opposition to such a large amount of land and to the removal of the high school from the center of town, the issue passed.

The new Mexico High School opened on January 23, 1928. The splendid building, ultramodern facilities and impressive location amid trees and rolling fields caught the attention of educators and civic leaders across the state. Some called it one of the most beautiful high school campuses in the nation.

The staff of the *1929 Mexicoan* boasted of their new school's special features: space for 1,500 students; 24 class rooms; 2 study halls; a good library; a large gymnasium; Emmons Hall, the auditorium; a cafeteria; 57 miles of electric wiring; plenty of playground space; a lake; a quarter-mile track; Hawthorne Heights, the football field; two tennis courts; bluffs, woodland, trees "and—possibilities!"

With the opening of the new high school elementary children moved into McMillan, and North Side finally closed. The battered old building was sold and used for commercial purposes until it was torn down in the late 1950s.

Expansion continued. Within ten years, despite the Depression, the school board, with a federal grant and financial support from A. P. Green, made plans for a $92,000 elementary school to replace the aging South Side. The new red-brick building on West Boulevard, named Eugene Field School, opened in 1936. At the same time an $87,000 addition and extensive improvements were made at Garfield.

Always conscious of potential overcrowding, board members turned next to existing buildings at Hardin College. Numerous plans for this campus had fallen through since it closed in 1932; in 1939 the Board purchased its four buildings and eleven-acre grounds for $27,000. After massive remodeling, it opened in September 1940 as the city's first junior high school.

While World War II brought school construction across the nation to a standstill, in the postwar years the Mexico Board faced, as Superintendent Hawthorne put it, "a rapid mushroom growth of the schools." Reflecting the addition of rural students, in 1955 new classrooms were being added at Eugene Field, and two new elementary schools opened. One, in the city's northwest area, was named Hawthorne in honor of the longtime superintendent. The other, in the northeast, carried on the name of McMillan. The original McMillan, now referred to as Central, would serve for district offices and at times for extra classrooms over the next decade.

In the meantime, integration was being implemented in the district. Beginning in 1954, with no major problems, Garfield students entered first the high school—44 blacks among 575 whites—and then Hardin Junior High and the grade schools. Later Garfield itself served all the district's sixth graders, closing for good in 1975.

With enrollment still rising due to integration, to the addition of high school students from St. Brendan's Catholic School, and to the continuing influx from the rural schools, the board continued to implement a program of expansion. Under the leadership of a new superintendent, L. Buford Thomas, a large addition to the high school was completed in 1962. The year 1964 saw new classrooms at McMillan, Hawthorne and Eugene Field. In 1968 the Vocational and Technical School was built—on the high school campus, but separate from that building; it would later be named in honor of its first director, Davis Hart. A new middle school for grades six, seven and eight would open in 1975 on the site of the old Fair Grounds, leaving the district offices and special educational programs on the Hardin campus.

Buildings alone, however, give an incomplete picture of the public school system; of paramount importance were its people. For fifty years the expanding district reflected the leadership of L. B. Hawthorne. Since his arrival in Mexico in 1902, he had served as teacher, principal, superintendent and elected member of the school board—a career as an educator spanning a full half-century. Not without opposition at times, he nevertheless earned the respect of faculty, administrators and community residents. At his death in 1967 former school board member Mrs. O. P. James, expressing the thoughts of many, said: "Those of us who worked officially with Mr. Hawthorne . . . have often realized since how far he looked to the future and how wisely he led the community toward providing good schools for Mexico. In Mr. Hawthorne we knew greatness."

Members of the Board of Education over these middle decades— from the early 1920s to the early 1970s—were deeply involved in the district's continuing growth. Among them were Dr. A. C. White, Dr. Fred Griffin, William S. Eller, J. W. Buffington, Alan Coatsworth and Mrs. P. J. Null—the first woman on the Board, elected to seven terms. Still others included Mrs. Sallie Mays Ekern, James F. Cooper, Jackson Wright, Warren O. McIntyre, Carl Burchfield, William B. Nowell, Dr. Ben Jolly and Dr. Frank Sutton.

And then there were the teachers.

Some teachers served as school principals: Mrs. Laura Hoagland at South Side; Miss Annie Bledsoe at Eugene Field; Esque Douglas and Mrs. Quinnie Benton at Garfield; Miss Jennie Karnes at McMillan Elementary; Miss Virginia Botts at McMillan, both old and new; Ross Ferris at Hardin Junior High; J. T. Angus, Clarence Mackey and William E. Lowry at the High School.

Other teachers reigned in the classroom. The community would long remember most with gratitude—for their years of devotion to their children, for the colorful influence of their personalities, for their forceful leadership and for the learning they inspired.

Students would long remember their own teachers, calling their names with varying degrees of respect, approval and even fondness: . . . Miss Wright . . . Miss Houston . . . Mr. Gorrell . . . Miss Bickley . . . Miss Denham . . . Miss Ward . . . Miss Creigh . . . Miss Carter . . . Miss Gibbs . . . Miss Bride . . . Coach Craig . . . Mrs. DeVault . . . Mrs. Des Combes . . . Coach Muir . . . Miss Baker . . . Mr. Willer . . . Mrs. Webster. . . . During the century's middle years these and a host of other dedicated teachers graced the classrooms of the Mexico School District.

Assignments on those blackboards long since have been erased, the voices of those students long hushed. But from the routine of those days emerge shared experiences of school: first graders saying the ABCs, young hearts pledging allegiance to the American Flag, teachers' frowns that meant no talking, the smells of lunch time, the anxious wait for a report card, the heavy silence of a test, seniors marching to commencement, Friday afternoon's final bell, the roar of support at a basketball game, an autumn moon rising over homecoming court and football team. . . .

Impressions of school, the common bond.

42

On Sunday Morning

On Sunday morning, in the middle years of the twentieth century, towns and communities across Audrain County assumed a customary pattern of Sabbath stillness and solitude.

In Mexico the Square stood vacant. At South Jefferson and Liberty the city's lone stoplight flashed idly on empty streets. Only an occasional car rumbled over brick pavement nearby. Now and then a train, deafening in the absence of normal weekday bustle, shrieked to a stop. Pedestrians were scarce. All stores and businesses stood closed; later in the day a gas station or two might open, along with the Liberty and Rex Theaters. At the Hotel Hoxsey, the two railroad depots, the fire station and the Jefferson Café a handful of people went about their jobs. Life's everyday routine hung suspended, muffled in the silence that settled across town.

Sunday morning. It was welcomed by most residents as a time for rest, for recovering from the past week's work—and for church. More than a third of the town's ten thousand souls would be present during the day at church, and many of the rest would somehow feel they ought to be. In their best clothes and on best behavior, children made their way to Sunday School. Adults—men in suits, white shirts and neckties, ladies in dresses, hats and gloves—headed for morning worship service. Church bells pealed, a reminder of the day and of the importance in their lives of their religion.

Religion, like education, trailed west into Audrain County along with its early settlers. On Sunday mornings in the 1830s and 1840s Christians met in various places for worship: a convenient grove of trees, the home of a fellow believer, the Court House, or the town's small meetinghouse. On some Sundays, and on random Saturdays and weekday afternoons as well, people traveled ten or twelve miles to hear a particular speaker or to attend "meeting."

In general those gathering for these simple worship services heard scripture readings, recited a psalm or Bible verses from memory, repeated the Lord's Prayer and listened to a "discourse" from one of their own or a sermon from a visiting preacher. Often they stayed for a funeral or a wedding at the close of preaching, and at times for a "love feast," or communion. There was little music; to many such a "frill" was deemed sinful. Sometimes, depending on the congregation, a few would join in as a strong voice lifted in the familiar strains of an old hymn such as "Guide Me, O Thou Great Jehovah, Pilgrim in this barren land . . ."

Strongly Protestant, these Christians went by many names: Methodists, Old School Baptists, Reformers, Regular Baptists, Cumberland Presbyterians, Iron-Side Baptists, Campbellites, Disciples of Christ, Calvinists. Not every adult was automatically considered to be a "Christian"; usually this term was reserved for active church members. Uppermost in the minds of individuals and preachers alike were such topics as original sin, infant baptism, immersion, the power of evil, damnation of the soul, predestination, church discipline, the temperance movement, the rewards of hard work and who had come forward at the last meeting.

Audrain's first settlers were mostly Methodists and Baptists. The former as early as 1832 were meeting in the home of John Martin, and the latter at the home of Ackley Day. This Missionary Baptist group organized in 1836 with fifteen members, including one colored servant, and soon built the Hopewell Baptist Church a mile or so southwest of the Court House on the Mexico-Columbia Road—the first church in the county. One of their members, William Morgan Jesse, became renowned throughout the area as a powerful preacher, the first of several in his family.

Gradually other congregations organized, some out in the county and several in or near Mexico. Methodists built the first church in town in 1838, in the block west of Jefferson, on the south side of Promenade Street. Two years later a group branching off from the Hopewell assembly built the Davis Fork Regular Baptist Church. This small meetinghouse, used also for a school, was located a block from the Square on the west side of North Washington. For years it served other groups as well as Baptists.

About the same time the Disciples of Christ organized, in 1853 building a small frame church on the north side of Liberty at Water Street. Facing south toward "virgin prairie," this building had two front doors, one on either side of the pulpit; women entered and sat on the east, men on the west. Dedicated in 1854, the first sermon in the church was preached by M. Y. Duncan, a young schoolteacher.

The fourth Mexico church in existence before the Civil War was the Presbyterian. With earlier attempts proving unsuccessful, it officially organized in 1851. By 1856 the congregation was constructing a church on the south side of Promenade, east of Coal, at a cost of $6,000.

After the war other denominations formed. The Roman Catholics first built a small church known as St. Stephen's, and then in 1874, at the corner of Breckenridge and Clark, a larger building to be called St. Brendan's. St. Paul's Episcopal Church went up in 1870 at the northwest corner of Promenade and Clark. By 1884 the Lutheran congregation had begun to meet in homes and within a few years had built at North Olive and Orange. Three major churches served the black community: the Methodist Episcopal, at the southwest corner of Jackson and Western; the African Methodist, on the north side of Liberty and East Trinity; and the Second Baptist, on the north side of West Elm and Railroad. During these years the first Baptist and Methodist congregations each built a new house of worship at Coal and Promenade. All of these churches were modest plain buildings, unpretentious in style, with little in the way of adornment.

Around the turn of the century, with a rising population and better economic conditions, several Mexico congregations began to plan larger and more elaborate buildings. Reflecting trends across the Midwest, these new churches were generally of brick, in a modified Gothic style characterized by turrets, domes and stained glass windows. Interiors were often wood-paneled, with dark red carpeting, cushioned pews, carved wood pulpits and lecterns, choir lofts and, a radical change for some, pipe organs.

While the Disciples of Christ moved in 1905 to a new site at the northeast corner of West Jackson and Olive to build their new church, others remained at their same locations. As early as 1894 the First Baptists were constructing a second church on their lot at the northwest corner of East Promenade and Coal. In 1898 Presbyterians built a large yellow-brick edifice at that southeast corner, and in 1902 the Methodists followed with their new building at the southwest corner. On Sunday mornings this intersection overflowed with worshippers and soon became known as "Church Corner."

Activities for these congregations during the early 1900s centered around weekly worship service, Sunday School, men's study groups, church dinners, women's missionary societies, daily vacation Bible school, youth fellowship, revival meetings and, on Sunday evenings and often Wednesday nights as well, prayer meetings. Organs were put to good use; choirs and congregations sang with fervor such hymns as "Onward Christian Soldiers" and "God of Our Fathers, whose Almighty Hand."

Over the next half-century, through World War I, the Depression and World War II, the customary activities of these churches continued, reflecting the importance of religion in the life of the community. With the postwar years of the late 1940s and 1950s churches across the nation as well as in Audrain saw an increase in membership and attendance.

In January of 1950 Mexico was featured in a *Life* magazine article on churches in a typical Midwestern small city. Statistics cited showed the First Baptist as the largest congregation with 1,300 members, the Methodists next with 1,150, followed by the Christians with 917, the Roman Catholics with 850, Presbyterians with 550, Lutherans with 100 and several smaller groups. On a typical January Sunday in that year those attending worship services at the town's seventeen churches totaled 3,428.

Sermons during these years emphasized not current events or the "social gospel," but a personal relationship with God, the wages of sin, the concept of hell and damnation, the importance of prayer and the necessity of bringing God's word to church members and to the rest of the world.

Change, however, was coming to American society and to religion. Even these small Midwestern congregations would soon be engulfed in national problems and evolving moral issues: the use of atomic power, the threat of communism, war in Korea, a rising divorce rate, juvenile delinquency, segregation, consumerism and an affluent lifestyle and changes in the traditional family. Over the 1960s and 1970s many Americans would begin to alter the place in their lives held by religion; Audrain Countians would be no exception.

In the meantime, for Mexico and Audrain, Sunday morning remained a time for rest, relaxation and church.

43

MMA on Parade

T he founding of the Missouri Military Academy marks a proud page in the history of Mexico and Audrain County. Initial steps to provide the area with a good private school for young men were taken in 1889. More than a century later it continues to prosper.

Colonel A. F. Fleet, veteran of the Confederate Army, graduate of the University of Virginia and currently a professor at the University of Missouri, had widely publicized his interest in organizing such a school. When a group of Mexico citizens contacted him and offered support for a private military academy, he agreed to head the institution. Charles H. Hardin, former governor of Missouri and founder of Hardin College, generously supported the project, extending financial aid and leadership for the community's efforts.

Amid predictions that it would have "the grandest future of any school in the state," residents of the area opened their hearts and their pocketbooks for the new venture. Adding to Governor Hardin's initial donation of $1,000, supporters gave amounts ranging from $2.50 to $500. The bulk of the fund amassed for the project came from over forty contributors pledging $100 each for "the Finest Military School Buildings in the West."

The desired twenty acres of land and $15,000—eventually to rise to $25,000—were quickly obtained. A site was selected on West Boulevard, just east of the Fair Grounds, and plans were made under Fleet's direction for brick buildings of gothic style architecture. The community, aware of the advantages of having Hardin College in their midst, now cooperated in every way for the success of the new "male school." The Academy owed its beginnings, said an early catalog, "to the liberality and public spirit of the citizens of Mexico, Missouri."

The new Missouri Military Academy opened its doors on Tuesday, September 16, 1890. More than sixty young men from Missouri, Kansas, Kentucky, Texas and the Indian Territory were enrolled, with a substantial number from Mexico and the county. A faculty carefully selected for its intellectual strength as well as its military background was drawn from across the South and Midwest. It quickly became known as an institution of academic excellence with emphasis upon discipline.

All went well until September 24, 1896. Reported the *Mexico Intelligencer:*

> Last night the fire fiend held high carnival in Mexico, and today, as a result of that orgie, the stately and imposing group of buildings which composed the Missouri Military Academy are a smoldering mass of ruins, and all that remains of that institution, which was a pride and joy to our people, are some charred and blackened walls.

Fortunately, although there were injuries, the fire caused no loss of life. But the Academy closed. Colonel Fleet, responding to an offer of buildings in a small Indiana town, departed within days, taking most of the cadets and faculty with him. Academy supporters in Mexico were left to struggle with the fire's aftermath.

With the aid of the local Business Men's Association and under the leadership of A. K. Yancey, president of Hardin College, and W. D. Fonville, superintendent of the Alabama Military Institute, efforts began to rebuild the Academy. Convinced of its value and importance to the community, civic leaders "most cheerfully and promptly" donated once again to the institution.

A new site was selected on the eastern edge of town at Bellevue Place, which offered "an elegant blue-grass Campus" ideal for a military school. The new buildings, of a simple and more classic design, soon became visible across the empty fields at the east end of Promenade Street. After a recess of four years, MMA opened again on September 20, 1900.

With Colonel Fonville at its head, the school gradually gained strength academically. It soon became a post of the Missouri National Guard and was recognized by the U.S. War Department. The caliber of its cadets steadily rose as it became recognized throughout the Midwest for its Christian environment, the integrity of its faculty and the high quality of its students' academic performance.

In 1911 Fonville resigned, turning the school over to Colonel Walter R. Kohr; three years later the board of trustees chose Colonel E. Y. Burton as its president. During his tenure, after years of intense effort and stiff competition, the War Department named MMA "an Honor Military school," one of only ten in the nation. It was a major achievement for the Academy, one that would be carefully guarded over the coming decades.

During the Depression of the 1930s schools across the nation suffered. The formation of a new corporation for the Academy in 1933 brought it under the leadership of Colonel C. R. Stribling Jr. He was another Virginian, a faculty member since 1920 and a staunch MMA supporter. Five other stockholders joined him in administering the school: Marquess Wallace, R. H. Linneman, Alden Brown, Tony B. Lumpkin and O. G. Hocker. They were able to save the school financially and to maintain its position as a superior military academy.

Another major change in its administration took place in 1948 when MMA was reorganized as a non-profit educational corporation. Continuing as president was Colonel Stribling. He would remain in that position for another two decades and then serve on the Board of Trustees until his death in 1983. In 1968 the Board selected as president his son, Charles R. Stribling, III, the first alumnus to head the school.

Over the decades the Academy continued to maintain its rank as an outstanding military school with emphasis upon discipline and scholastic achievement. In June, 1985, it was recognized by the U.S. Department of Education as "an Exemplary Private School," one of sixty-five across the nation and the only military school so honored. At special ceremonies at the White House an Excellence in Private Education Flag was presented by President Ronald Reagan to Colonel Stribling. That fall an elated cadet corps stood at attention as the new flag ascended the MMA flagpole.

Through the years the people of Mexico followed closely the events at the Academy. The cadets, individually and as a group, excelled in music, sports, debate and journalism as well as in military and academic endeavors. The corps marched in local parades as well as in gubernatorial and presidential inaugural ceremonies. The Fusileers, Band and Drum and Bugle Corps performed at numerous functions and at times were seen on national television. The town remained proud of its Academy.

When MMA marked its centennial in 1989 the entire community joined its faculty, alumni and friends in celebrating a century of exceptional progress. The cadets had followed well their charge to "Look like a soldier; Act like a gentleman." And the Academy was, in its one-hundredth year, still "a pride and joy to our people."

Mexico and Audrain extended congratulations and their own twenty-one-gun salute.

44

In the Pages of the *Ledger*

$\mathbb{F}$or the better part of the county's first one hundred and fifty years many Mexico and Audrain residents got their news from the White family's *Mexico Ledger*. Under their leadership the *Ledger* informed, instructed, influenced—and even, at times, infuriated— readers from 1876 to 1986.

The first newspaper established in the county, in 1855, was the *Missouri Weekly Ledger*. It was published in Mexico every Saturday, at a cost listed as "$1 in Advance" for the year. Its circulation, limited mostly to the town, was small—probably less than three or four hundred. Calling it politically neutral its founder, John B. Williams, proclaimed its devotion to "Literature, Science, Agriculture, Education, Amusements, the Markets, etc."

Located, along with Dobyn's Grocery, in a building at the southeast corner of the Square on what later would become the Ringo lot, the paper was destroyed by fire in 1861 and temporarily ceased publication. After a lapse of three years its few assets—and there were no files—went to a new owner, who briefly published the *Mexico Messenger*. Sold again, another owner changed its politics to "Democrat" and its name back to the *Ledger*.

Over the following decades the town saw the rise and fall of two dozen or so attempts at a newspaper. A variety of editors and political views, but a common difficulty in making a go of a small town paper, marked them all. They included the *Audrain County Banner*, the *Audrain County Signal*, the *Beacon*, the *Gazette* and the *Expositor*. One writer noted that there had been many and varied attempts to keep the public informed: ". . . greenback papers, Republican papers and nondescript papers . . ."

The tall narrow columns of these early newspapers, with their small print and subdued headlines, had access to only limited national news, with some items being weeks old. They were filled, instead, with editorial comment, advertisements, jokes, testimonials, dissertations, serial stories, poetry and letters or responses to readers. Local news varied with the aims of the editor and his capacity to be on the scene of any unfolding event.

Surviving Mexico's stiff competition, tight economy and varied politics over the years would be two newspapers. The *Beacon* changed hands in 1866, becoming known briefly as the *Mexico Ledger* before it was bought in 1872 by Colonel J. E. Hutton and renamed the *Mexico Weekly Intelligencer*. Four years later R. M. White bought the original *Missouri Ledger,* keeping its newer name, the *Mexico Ledger*.

The *Intelligencer* and the *Ledger* were not, however, without competition. Notable among other newspapers in the county were the *Vandalia Leader*, established in 1872 (and still operating in the 1980s); the *Martinsburg Monitor*, dating, under other names, from 1907; the *Laddonia Herald*, established in 1884, and others. The two Mexico firms continued, the *Intelligencer* finally shutting down its presses in the 1940s, leaving the *Ledger* as the city's only daily newspaper.

Back in 1876 Robert M. White was a recent graduate of Westminster College. His grandson once described him as then being a "tall, gangling, hard-working, fast-walking, plain-spoken young fellow." Offered a playing position with the St. Louis Browns' baseball club, he had declined, choosing instead to enter the world of journalism. He paid $1,000 for the twenty-one-year-old newspaper that was then known officially as the *Mexico Ledger*.

Full of enthusiasm, White published his first issue on September 21, 1876. Under the masthead he ran his motto: "To Our Pride in the Past and Our Hope for the Future, Let Us Add Vigorous Work, in the Living Present." He also stated his intention, among other goals, to "avoid all personalities and needless pitching into our friends and neighbors."

Determined to increase the paper's circulation, then well below one thousand, he set up his office in the Ledger Building at the northwest corner of the Square. During these struggling early years he served not only as editor and proprietor but also, according to one *Ledger* article, as "reporter, copy reader, head writer, proof reader, makeup man, bookkeeper and advertising solicitor." Gradually he captured a number of loyal readers.

Beginning in 1886, White published the paper as a daily, while continuing the weekly edition (which would last until 1956). By the turn of the century the circulation of the weekly was five times what it had been when he took over, and the *Daily Ledger* was thriving.

In explaining his political and editorial stands, White once said, "I am for the things that will help my town and people." He gained a reputation as a "stemwinder," his editorials attacking his foes and defending with vigor his beliefs. He became an avid booster of Mexico and Audrain County, taking a leading role in promoting its economic, political, civic and social progress. His stands on current projects were clearly stated, as were his political beliefs and endorsements. In 1885 a Warrensburg newspaper editor, in an unusual comment for this age of cut-throat journalism, wrote about him: "Bob White's paper . . . has done more for the town of Mexico than all of its citizens combined. The Ledger is to Mexico what the heart is to man."

For sixty years White, now addressed by many as "Colonel," upheld the high standards of the *Ledger.* In 1917 he turned the paper over to his son, remaining a strong influence until his death in 1934.

Taking over the enterprise was L. Mitchell White. Very much a part of the newspaper world, he had begun his career at the *Ledger* at the age of twelve. After graduation from Westminster College and a short apprenticeship at the *Denver Post*, he returned to Mexico, from then on to be known as "Mitch White of the *Ledger.*"

A respected journalist in his own right, the second of the family dynasty shaped the *Mexico Evening Ledger,* as it was now called, through the 1920s, the Depression, World War II and the postwar era. Through these years it met with increasing financial success and journalistic acclaim. Since the turn of the century it had enjoyed a reputation as one of the best "country" newspapers in the state. Now it would be called by those in the profession "one of the nation's finest small newspapers."

As editor and proprietor from 1910 to 1965, Mitchell White held strong opinions and had a direct way of stating them. Excerpts from two editorials published in a 1976 *Ledger* commemorative issue reveal something of his style and beliefs:

Feb. 18, 1933: Backscratching by politicians is one thing that will interfere with cutting costs in government. The politicians know that something should be done, but they want to do the impossible, which is to save money without stepping on each others' toes.

Aug. 27, 1942: We don't care how large Mexico grows if we can keep those fine spiritual ideals and cling tirelessly to those lasting fundamentals that make for friendly living and wholesome community life. We are not worshipping any goldplated idols nor is any leather-lunged demagog directing our thinking.

The third of the White family to operate the *Ledger* enterprise was Robert M. White II. He began his career as a reporter after service in World War II, returning to Mexico and the paper in 1945. He assumed a management role after 1946.

Recognized as an excellent journalist, he continued the tradition of the family newspaper from the 1950s into the 1980s; he became editor and publisher in 1965 following the death of his father. During these years circulation increased from 4,000 to 12,000 across what he came to call "Ledgerland." He also continued the family tradition of winning numerous awards for journalistic excellence—"enough blue ribbons," wrote a St. Louis newspaper once, "to swath the office in bunting."

In the spring of 1986, however, in the face of changing times and difficult circumstances for smaller family-owned newspapers across the nation, White announced the sale of the *Ledger*. Readers reacted with surprise and dismay. While the paper would continue, no member of the White family would be involved in its publication.

The three generations of White editors and their *Mexico Ledger* were a powerful voice in Mexico. They promoted the progress of city and county, shaped their character, applauded their successes and guided their political direction—for many years almost exclusively Democratic. While not always on the winning side and regarded by some as biased, their participation in and concern for the betterment of the county and its people characterized their efforts over the paper's more than one hundred years. Through its pages can be traced, day by day, much of the history of Mexico and Audrain County.

Readers regarded the *Ledger* as an important part of daily life. They turned by habit to news, obituaries, hospital reports, the weather forecast and the sports page. They read editorials and political endorsements. They checked on election returns, business developments, county court meetings, city council meetings and school board meetings. They followed farm reports and the stock market. They looked for news about neighbors and organizations. They read the society page with its write-ups on bridge clubs, book clubs, women's clubs, church circles, teas, luncheons, dinners, showers, trips, visiting relatives, birthday parties and anniversary celebrations.

And, with scissors in hand, they watched for engagement announcements, wedding accounts, birth notices, school articles and pictures of their children . . . finding a record of their lives in the pages of the *Ledger*.

45

The Changing of the Square

The middle years of the twentieth century brought much change to America—to its society and government, its cities, towns and farms, and its people. From the 1940s into the 1970s and 1980s Audrain County, like the nation, saw many aspects of change. Her people experienced the disruption of individual lives, the decline of customary ways of living and the disappearance of much that was familiar and comfortable. Coming more rapidly and more deeply than in previous times, change and adjustment affected everyone. People faced new demands, new lifestyles, new opportunities. Change came everywhere, even to the Square.

War brought the most obvious change. Audrain men served in Italy and Normandy, the Philippines and Iwo Jima, Korea and Vietnam. Faraway places and the turmoil of war forever changed their lives. Civilians at home met the demands of wartime with hard work, restraint and personal sacrifice, their horizons, too, expanding and their lives undergoing change. Some left home for other locations; many took on new jobs. Of necessity the county adapted to a world made smaller, her people affected by events far, far indeed from the Square.

Postwar years, too, brought change. Everyday life was not the same. Across the nation and in Audrain County people welcomed a rising standard of living and an abundance of consumer goods. As they became available and affordable new automobiles, washing machines, air conditioners, dishwashers and television sets were in demand, producing different lifestyles.

Smaller "nuclear families" demanded smaller homes. Mexico in the late 1940s and 1950s faced a crucial lack of housing. With the areas known as Little Oklahoma and Trolley Heights now declining, new neighborhoods were developed east of North Jefferson, out near the Fair Grounds, and west along Kentucky Road. One-floor ranch-style houses sprang up. Sidewalks, wrought-iron fences and front porch swings gave way to open backyards, picture windows, patios and barbecue grills.

Schoolchildren met change, as the 1950s brought not only new classrooms but a renewed emphasis upon education. Better roads, transportation by school bus and larger buildings brought school consolidation. The county's rural schools, once numbering nearly a hundred, gradually closed. Kindergarten became compulsory and preschools, some church-supported, opened. By the 1970s teachers everywhere were facing change: new curricula and lower academic standards; discipline problems and an increasing lack of respect; the effects of divorce, juvenile delinquency and teenage pregnancy and the impact of drugs. Children were growing up earlier.

County government changed. The old Court House, long regarded as too small, outdated and a firetrap, succumbed to a vote and the wrecking ball; to the distress of many it was torn down in 1950, its old clock fading into history. A plainer, modern three-story brick building costing a half-million dollars went up on the same site. The county court became the county commission, its members no longer "judges" but "commissioners."

The political scene shifted. Long a staunch stronghold of the Democratic Party, county residents began to see Republican names on local ballots and to elect some to office—Pete Todsen as a commissioner was the first. Nationally, beginning in 1968 with the election of Richard Nixon, the county often voted Republican in presidential elections, while backing Democrats in the U.S. Senate and their 9th U.S. House District.

During the next decade one of Audrain's own was elected to high office. After becoming state auditor in a remarkable 1970 landslide victory, in 1972 and again in 1980, Republican Christopher S. (Kit) Bond, grandson of A. P. Green, was elected Governor of Missouri, and in 1986, U.S. Senator. This paved the way for even greater political diversity in the county. Despite the continuing dominance of Democrats at the courthouse, Circuit Judge Edward D. Hodge (elected in 1976) and Recorder of Deeds Virginia Pehle (elected in 1982) were Republicans. Audrain became, in the eyes of many, a two-party county.

Although population increased statewide during the 1940s, 1950s and 1960s, Audrain was the only county in northeast Missouri to show such growth. While Mexico grew proportionately, some towns did not. These years saw the decline of Molino, Rowena, Thompson, Rush Hill, Skinner and Worcester with Vandalia, Laddonia, Farber, Martinsburg and Benton City more or less holding their own. By 1970 the county's population leveled out at just over twenty-five thousand, and that of the county seat at around twelve thousand and would hover there over the next two decades.

Change came to the county's farms. While Audrain remained a leading agricultural county, with over 90 percent of her land in farms, the nature of those farms was changing. Their number declined, from just under twenty-five hundred in the early 1930s to fifteen hundred by 1970. They increased in size, in 1935 averaging 174 acres and by 1970, 266. Farmers were plagued by financial problems; many young men looked elsewhere for work.

Crops changed. Introduced into Audrain in the 1920s by Mexico High School "Ag-teacher" Alphonse Gorrell, soybeans became its leading crop. Milo, too, now grew beside fields of corn and wheat. Fewer chickens were raised, and more livestock. Fewer mules and horses were seen, and more tractors. In the mid-1960s the Fair ceased to be. Good saddle horses were still bred locally but only a few trainers—and eventually only one, Art Simmons—carried on that tradition. In general Audrain farmers adapted well to irrigation, mechanization, diversification, agribusiness and other approaches to modern agriculture. Despite change, the county's farms remained a primary strength.

The railroad, long vital to Audrain, declined. Two lines remained, but with fewer trains, and down on Mexico's South Jefferson Street warning lights replaced the longtime "crossing man." Though roads improved, interurban bus lines stopped operating, bowing to the family car. "Motor freight carriers" handled local trade as three main highways and the nearby interstate strengthened the trucking industry. The Mexico Airport grew in importance, gradually expanding.

Local business changed. In Mexico the International Shoe Factory, long a leading source of jobs, closed. Grocery stores gave way to supermarkets like Kroger's and IGA; no longer could housewives ring up Moore's for groceries delivered to the back door. Home milk delivery stopped. Ice plants closed. The Fredendall & Wilkins Department Store, with its metal change boxes hurtling along ceiling tracks straight to clerk and customer, went out of business, unable to compete with cheaper goods and modern sales methods. Woolworth's Five and Dime did the same. Drugstores became pharmacies and, except for Rexall's, no longer housed a soda fountain.

The city's oldest family-owned business, Crown Linen, dating back to 1891, expanded, now serving commercial establishments across northeast Missouri. Pilcher's Jewelry Store, a town fixture since 1867;

Wonneman's Flowers, except for a short interruption, since the 1890s; Pearl Motor Company, selling cars since 1918; and Hagan's Clothing, on the Square since 1934, were among the retail stores that endured. The Missouri Farmers Association's Soybean Plant prospered, as did the Missouri Livestock Market Center and the Baker Meat Packing Company, attracting farmers from across the county and beyond. The hospital and Missouri Military Academy began to list the largest number of employees in the area. The *Ledger,* reaching its century mark under the White family, continued to cover the news "like the dew covers Little Dixie."

The Mexico Savings Bank evolved into the Commerce Bank, with three locations in town. The First National Bank moved from South Jefferson to East Liberty, and new financial institutions, real estate agencies and insurance companies opened.

New business appeared. Wetterau, Missouri's largest food distributor, moved a central office to Mexico. Entrepreneurs promoted the production of plastic goods. New stores sold electronic equipment and computers. Flat Rock gave way to the West Plaza Shopping Center and empty fields to Wal-Mart and South Trails, establishing new buying patterns that boosted the economy but drew business away from the Square.

The brick plants continued to be the major industries in the county. Both Green's and Mexico Refractories, however, saw changes in name and management. Still supplying a world market, the fire brick industry itself evolved into the manufacture of a variety of refractories products. Residents noted with pride that Audrain refractory workers helped make possible the nation's space program and man's walk on the moon.

The city of Mexico saw major change. In 1949 it adopted the council-manager form of government; with this came improvements in streets, sewers, garbage collection and traffic patterns. City limits were extended. A special commission expanded and enhanced the city's parks and playground areas. Urban renewal plans, with public housing units, were implemented. Community development projects included two railroad underpasses and remedies for the perennially troublesome town branch. Parking meters came in during the late 1930s and 1940s and, by the 1980s, went out. The old city hall at the southwest corner of Jefferson and Promenade was razed, and the brick building at Love and Coal purchased for city offices. Fire and Police Departments combined into Public Safety.

In 1955 Mexico was chosen an All American City; another two decades and it would win acclaim as a National Tree City. Efforts of the Junior Chamber of Commerce and friends brought the Miss Missouri Pageant to town, along with many visitors and much good publicity. The Mexico Area Chamber of Commerce diligently promoted both city and county.

During these years a number of Audrain Countians were recognized far beyond the county's boundaries. Lt. Commander Samuel G. Fuqua, born and raised in Laddonia, was awarded the Congressional Medal of Honor for heroism and distinguished conduct aboard the *U.S.S. Arizona* during the 1941 Japanese attack on Pearl Harbor. Adolph J. Paschang, from Martinsburg, served as a missionary and then as Catholic bishop of a large area of war-torn China, becoming known as the "Little Bishop of Charity."

William Hirth, from Rush Hill, played a leading role in the organization of the Missouri Farmers' Association during the 1920s and 1930s. Joe Sunnen, who began in the 1940s, with his brother Gus, as an inventor of automotive and industrial products, by the 1970s was known internationally as a self-made millionaire industrialist and philanthropist. Two women in high academic circles received national recognition: Dr. Anna Jane Harrison in chemistry and Dr. Mary Alice Parrish as a professor and leader in political affairs.

These middle decades saw others step out on a larger, national stage. In the 1950s Walter G. Staley Jr. competed as an equestrian in three Olympic games, winning a bronze medal, and represented the United States at the Pan American Games in Mexico City, winning the gold. In the 1960s local attorney Jackson A. Wright served as president of the Missouri Bar Association. William S. Lowe, chief executive officer at A. P. Green Firebrick Company, in 1972 was elected president of the U.S. Chamber of Commerce. In 1986 Dr. H. Peter Ekern became president of the Missouri State Medical Association. For years G. Andy Runge held a leadership role across the state in matters of Republican politics, conservation and higher education. Numerous others contributed as well, in many fields.

More professional people settled in the community. Doctors, dentists and attorneys, including several women, left second-floor offices on the Square in favor of new one-floor, easily accessible buildings. In the wake of a court case drawing national attention the Audrain Hospital successfully bridged differences between osteopaths and medical doctors; it expanded, not once but again and again, becoming the Audrain Medical Center.

"Church Corner" was no more, as first the Baptists and then the Presbyterians moved from Coal and Promenade, leaving only the Methodists with their large new building at that corner. The number of congregations in Mexico climbed to nearly three dozen as church attendance rose through the 1950s; many built in new neighborhoods. Changes in moral values, behavior patterns and ethical responsibility during the 1960s and 1970s challenged all churches, as did the decline in membership that began in the 1970s.

Hotels disappeared, the Jefferson and the Alamo, the former Ben Bolt, closing. The Hotel Hoxsey with its elegant Gold Room became mostly apartments and in 1980 burned to the ground, killing six people. After the Air Park went up east of town in 1950, other motels were built. Nursing homes and retirement centers opened. The city and county welcomed the Missouri Veterans' Home.

Young and old patronized Eddie's Drive-In and the A&W Root Beer Stand, eventually acquiring a taste also for store-fried chicken and pizza. A drive-in movie opened east of town. After sixty years the once-posh Liberty Theater closed in 1982; movie fans now frequented the smaller three-cinema building in the shopping center.

KXEO Radio went on the air on December 3, 1948, KWWR-FM in 1966. Announcer Greg Swanson and newsman Jim Landry became familiar voices in Audrain homes as the station delivered national and local news, market reports, weather conditions, commercials, sports events and music—first the top forty, then rock and roll, and later country and western. Local television arrived in the late 1960s with the White family's See TV; among its welcome contributions: early returns on election night.

Fashions changed. People looked different. Men no longer sported vests, pocket watches or hats; longer hair and beards came in. Ladies exchanged corsets, gloves, obligatory hats and high heels for bouffant hairdos, mini-skirts and pant suits. Blue jeans, tennis shoes and T-shirts became the uniform for all ages.

Personal habits changed. As cigars and cigarettes declined, spittoons vanished and ashtrays dwindled. Soda cans and litter proliferated. Dieting became the rage and dieters were highly visible. Joggers appeared everywhere. People took up walking.

The times were changing—even for the Square.

Yet much remained of the Audrain County of yesterday. After a century and a half, residents continued to make it one of the best communities in the entire middle west. As always, it was a good place to raise children. Schools and churches and the library remained important. Every fire, emergency, or personal disaster never failed to bring forth generous financial aid, kind helping hands and sincere heartfelt prayers.

Times were changing.

But here and there small patches of prairie grass—though sparse—still sought the sun. Davis Fork still flowed to the Mississippi. And Audrain was still, for most of her people, their flourishing and proud county, not wanting in enterprise and spirit.

X

Notes and Index

Source Notes

The most important sources of information on the county's early history are the four following texts: S. M. Edwards, "History of Audrain County, Missouri," in *Illustrated Historical Atlas of Audrain Co., Missouri*, published in Philadelphia by Edwards Brothers of Missouri, in 1877; *History of Audrain County, Missouri*, published in St. Louis by the National Historical Company, in 1884, and reprinted in Mexico by the Audrain County Historical Society, in 1975; George Robertson, "History of Audrain County," in *A History of Northeast Missouri*, edited by Walter Williams and published in Chicago by Lewis Publishing Company, in 1913; and Herschel Schooley, *Centennial History of Audrain County*, published in Mexico by McIntyre Publishing Company, in 1937, and reprinted by the Audrain County Historical Society, in 1988.

These four sources as a whole cover the county's first century. Portions of some are duplicated in others; distinctions are not made in the following notes. Schooley in particular included many excerpts from the *Mexico Ledger*.

It should be noted that Robertson, prominent Audrain attorney and historian, pointed out in 1913 the absence of many early official county documents and court records. It is assumed that this was at least in part because of the confusion at the Court House during and after the Civil War. Such primary sources are therefore unavailable. Some, however, were quoted in the above histories and were therefore given appropriate consideration in this history.

In the Recorder's Office in the Audrain County Courthouse in Mexico are many original records related to land claims, deeds, plats, real estate transactions, marriage records, and so on. These were carefully researched and used in this history. The federal census records and other materials on microfilm, as well as other materials at the Mexico–Audrain County Library, were also of great benefit to this history. A major source of information was the morgue at the *Mexico Ledger,* including not only its own files but also some from the *Mexico Intelligencer*. The *Ledger* column "Yesterday in Mexico" has, over its numerous years, provided many facts, dates and details.

Of vital importance were the Audrain County Historical Society's files, records and artifacts. Some newspaper articles and other items could not be readily identified as to precise source or date because they were in scrapbooks or loose among letters and other items. These were used when they were obviously authentic and trustworthy. Letters, photographs, obituary notices, advertisements, scrapbooks filled with clippings and pictures and other such material, if deemed accurate, were relied upon to give a fuller history of the city and county. A primary source here was Susan B. Vanarsdale, "Diary, c. 1847–1855," an unpublished carbon of a typed manuscript in the Audrain County Historical Society files.

Of great significance because of its biographical entries as well as summaries of events, groups, businesses and so on, over more recent years, was *The History of Audrain County, Missouri: An Update, 1936–1986*, published in Mexico by the Audrain County Historical Society, in 1986.

For facts concerning the city of Mexico itself, various *City Directories* were referred to, such as for the years 1876, 1880, 1905. For town centennial histories of the other towns, see the respective towns: Laddonia, Molino, Vandalia, and so on. For the histories of the various churches, there are some interesting histories published by the churches themselves: Betty L. Baker, *Mexico Methodism*, published by the Methodist Church in 1976; M. Craig and M. Houston, *Lest We Forget*, published by the Christian Church in 1925; Leta Hodge, *A Legacy of Faith*, published by the Presbyterian Church in 1976; R. W. Luckaman and Patsy Luckaman, *A History of the Christian Church of Mexico, Missouri*, published by the Christian Church in 1987.

The newspapers referred to include the *Mexico Intelligencer*, the *Mexico Weekly Intelligencer*, the *Mexico Ledger*, the *Mexico Weekly Ledger* and the *Mexico Evening Ledger*. Also used were various yearbooks: *Ion*, of Hardin College, for the years 1900–1933, and *The McMillan*, of McMillan High School, for the years 1907–1927. Other sources are listed below.

Allison, Linda. *Annals of a Pioneer Doctor*. St. Louis, Mo.: C. B. Nicholson Printing, 1941.

Audrain, Frances Wendell. *We Begin with Peter Audrain*. Montrose, Calif.: Private printing, 1983.

Bryan, Wm. S., and Rose Robert. *A History of the Pioneer Families of Missouri*. St Louis, Mo.: Bryan, Brand and Company, 1876.

Burnham, W. Dean. *Presidential Ballots, 1836–1892*. Baltimore: Johns Hopkins University Press, 1955.

Downey, Bill. *Tom Bass, Black Horseman*. St Louis, Mo.: Saddles and Bridle, 1975.

Grant. U. S. *Personal Memoirs*. New York: Charles L. Webster and Co., 1885.

Green, Martha McHenry. *The Five Little Greens*. Mexico, Mo.: Martha M. G. Staley, 1985.

Hardin, Mary Barr. *Life and Writings of Governor Charles Henry Hardin*. St Louis, Mo.: Buschart Bros. Printers, 1896.

Hicks, John D. *The Federal Union: A History of the United States to 1865*. Cambridge, Mass.: Riverside Press, 1952.

Hill, John B. *The Presbytery of Kansas City and Its Predecessors*. Kansas City: Presbytery of Kansas City, 1901.

Hodge, Leta. *The Friend of Audrain: A History of Medicine in Audrain County*. Mexico, Mo.: Audrain Medical Center, 1985.

——. *Soldiers, Scholars, Gentlemen: The First Hundred Years of the Missouri Military Academy*. Mexico, Mo.: Missouri Military Academy, 1988.

McLaurin, Melton A. *Celia: A Slave*. Athens: University of Georgia Press, 1991.

Ohman, Marian M. *A History of Missouri's Counties, County Seats, and Courthouse Squares*. Columbia, Mo.: Curators of the University of Missouri, 1983.

Read, Orville H. *The Refractories People: A History of the A. P. Green Refractories Co*. Mexico, Mo.: A. P. Green Refractories Co., 1978.

Shoemaker, Floyd C., ed. *Missouri, Day by Day*. Columbia, Mo.: State Historical Society of MIssouri, 1942.

Standard Atlas of Mexico, Missouri. 1918.

Stevens, Walter B. *Centennial History of Missouri, II*. St Louis, Mo.: S. J. Clarke, 1921.

Chapter References

S ince this work was intended for the general reader, footnotes were not placed in the body of the text. Most of the material covering the county's first century is found in one or more of the four early county histories, as cited in the Bibliographic Essay above; distinctions are not made in these notes. Following are specific sources for information and quotes not so regarded or not clarified by the text. It should be noted that some sources cannot be clearly identified or dated.

I
Her Grand and Beautiful Prairie

Ch. 1   "fell and rose . . .": *History* (1884), 275.
        "contemplated county": *Laws of Missouri*, January 12, 1831, ch. 13.
Ch. 2   on Peter Audrain: Audrain, 30–32.
        the name Audrain: Robertson, 184
        the name Mexico: ibid., 186. See also Schooley, 18.
Ch. 3   "The territory . . .": Edwards.
        on Littleby: Bryan and Rose, 387–88.
        on Young: ibid., 388–89.
Ch. 4   voting story: *History* (1884), 178.
        "somewhat the sport . . .": ibid., 279.
Ch. 5   U.S. Land Patent, September 15, 1835, Cert. no. 4013.

II
Pioneers, Those Bold and Hardy Men

Ch. 6   "Be it remembered . . .": *History* (1884), 109.
        "On the motion . . .": ibid., 110.
        first road: ibid., 112.
        tax story: ibid., 283.
        "individual manhood . . .": ibid., 281.

Ch. 7	cases: ibid., 113–14.
	on Hall-Dingle fight: ibid., 187.
Ch. 8	on Shelbyville Square Plan: Ohman, 34.
	July 4, 1848: Vanarsdale.
Ch. 9	on culinary deliciousness: *History* (1884), 282.
	on early dances: ibid., 149–50.
Ch. 10	Christian Seminary: Craig and Houston, 11–13.

III
Our Flourishing and Proud County

Ch. 11	gold fever in county: *History* (1884), 348–50.
	"Off to Californy . . .": Hicks, 493.
	poem: *History* (1884), 350.
Ch. 12	on the grand duke: Schooley, 32.
Ch. 13	Callaway County killing: McLaurin.
	"Progress . . .": *City Directory, Mexico*, 1876.
	on 1860 Audrain vote: Burnham, 570.
Ch. 14	Grant quotes: Grant, 1:251–53.
Ch. 15	Lincoln order: Rev. R. S. Symington, in Hill, 220–21.

IV
Not Wanting in Enterprise and Spirit

Ch. 17	Quisenberry and family: letters from Lola Powell, 1958, 1960, in Audrain Co. Hist. Soc. files.
Ch. 18	statistics: *History* (1884), 195–96.
	numbers: "Yesterday in Mexico," September 7, 1885.
	general: Mexico Board of Education minutes.
Ch. 19	general: Hardin.
	grasshoppers: Stevens, 255–58.
	general: Shoemaker, 377, and speech to Audrain Co. Hist. Soc., n.d.
Ch. 20	general: *Mexico Ledger*, March 5, 1880, quoted in *History* (1884), 256–59.
	White quotes: Schooley, 27–28.

V
The Growing Metropolis of the Grand Prairie

Ch. 22   general: Schooley, 114–15.
    general: files, newspaper clippings, *Ledger* articles.
Ch. 23   general: interviews by author with L. B. Hawthorne, 1965–1966.
Ch. 24   on decor: "Yesterday in Mexico," August 5, 1878.
    fire: *Ledger* and *Intelligencer* articles, April 1918; comments, Caroline Worrell Gibbs, *Ledger*, December 18, 1993.
Ch. 25   on light: "Yesterday in Mexico," esp. September 14, 1885.

VI
A Progressive Agriculture County of Missouri

Ch. 26   on dresses: "Yesterday in Mexico," August 21, 1881.
Ch. 27   "perfect example . . .": Schooley, 105.
Ch. 28   general: files, records at Audrain Co. Hist. Soc.
Ch. 29   general: Hardin College catalogues, yearbooks.
Ch. 30   general: Clay; articles from *Intelligencer, Ledger, Laddonia Herald;* circuit court record, Lincoln County, October 19–23, 1903.

VII
Constantly Forging Ahead

Ch. 31   general: "Yesterday in Mexico," 1886.
Ch. 32   quote on McMillan: Schooley, 213.
    general: interviews by author with L. B. Hawthorne, 1965–1966.
Ch. 33   brochures, files, at Audrain Co. Hist. Soc.
    A. P. Green quote: Read, 14.
    Mexico Ledger Centennial Edition, 1936.
Ch. 34   on first Mexico hospital: A. P. Green, brief history in letter to Col. C. R. Stribling Jr., July 31, 1951.
    general: see Hodge, *Friend of Audrain.*
    ground-breaking quote: Judge D. H. Harris, speech, March 18, 1919.
Ch. 35   regulations: *Mexico City Directory*, 1892.

VIII
The Best Community in the Entire Middle West

Ch. 36   brochures, files Audrain Co. Hist. Soc.

Ch. 37   horses, cars and trollies: Schooley, 30.

Ch. 38   Mexico Telephone Co.: *Subscribers' Directory,* 1909.

Ch. 39   local statistics: *Mexico Ledger.*

Ch. 40   *Ledger Centennial Edition,* 1936.

                 Audrain Update, 331.

IX
With Indomitable Spirit

Ch. 42   1950 statistics: "A Sunday in Missouri," *Life Magazine,* January 23, 1950, 71–78.

Ch. 43   general: Hodge, *Soldiers, Scholars.*

Ch. 44   Schooley, 146–49.

                 Audrain Update, 256–57.

                 Mexico Ledger, September 21, 1976.

Ch. 45   agriculture: *Audrain Update,* 280–87.

Index

Audrain County Time Line

1801–09 *Jefferson*	**1803**	**Louisiana Purchase**
1809–17 *Madison*	1810 1812 1816	Skull Lick Massacre Territory of Missouri formed Littleby in county
1817–25 *Monroe*	**1821**	**Missouri becomes state** B. Young in county
1825–29 *J.Q.Adams*		
1829–37 *Jackson*	1831 1832 **1836**	"Contemplated County" set up Union School First Church: Hopewell Baptist **Mexico founded**: April 23 **Audrain County organized**: December 17
1837–41 *Van Buren*	**1837** 1838	**First County Court** First County-wide Election **First Court House** Methodist Church in Mexico
1841– *W.H.Harrison* 1841–45 *(Tyler)*	1840	First Census; Audrain pop. 1,949 First Presidential Election
1845–49 *Polk* 1849–50 *Taylor* 1850–53 *(Fillmore)*	1849 **1853**	Gold Rush **North Missouri Railroad**
1853–57 *Pierce*	1854 1857	**Thompson's Station** laid out Mexico incorporated **Martinsburg** laid out**Benton City** laid out
1857–61 *Buchanan*	1859 1860	Tom Bass born **First Audrain Fair**
1861–65 *Lincoln*	1861	Civil War begins Muldrow's Raid **U.S. Grant** arrives

1865–69	1865	Civil War ends
(A.Johnson)	1867	First bank in county: Mexico Savings
	1868	**Second Court House**
1869–1877	1870	First Mexico Board of Education
Grant	1871	**Vandalia** founded
		Laddonia founded
	1872	**Farber** founded
	1873	Hardin College founded
		First Mexico Public School
	1875	J.B.Morris dies
1877–81	1875–77	**C.H.Hardin** (Dem.) Governor of Missouri
Hayes	1876	*Mexico Ledger* under White
1881	1880	Execution of Kilgore
Garfield	1881	**Rush Hill** founded
1881–85	1885	First Electric Light Plant
(Arthur)		
1885–89		
Cleveland	1889	**MMA** founded
1889–93	1890–98	**G.B. Macfarlane** (Dem.) to Missouri Supreme Court
B.Harrison	1890	*Rex McDonald* foaled
	1892	First successful telephone company
1893–97		
Cleveland		
1897–1901	1896	MMA destroyed by fire
McKinley	1900	Pop. Audrain: 21,160; Mexico: 5,099
1901–05		MMA re-opens
(T.Roosevelt)	1902	Streets on Square paved with brick
		Rep. Rhodes Clay killed
1905–09	1908	McMillan H.S. accepts more rural 8th grade graduates
T.Roosevelt		
1909–13	**1910**	**A. P. Green Fire Brick Co.**
Taft		Audrain trolley line opens
	1913	**Mexico Hospital** opens
1913–21		**Mexico Carnegie Library** opens
Wilson		
	1918	World War I
		County hospital vote passes
		Ringo Hotel Fire
1921–23	1920	**Audrain Hospital** opens
Harding		
1923–25		
(Coolidge)		
1925–29	1927–47	**E.S.Gantt** (Dem.) to Missouri Supreme Court
Coolidge	1928	Wm. Hirth (b. Audrain) president, Missouri Farmers' Association
1929–33	1930	**J.B.Arthur: Mexico Refractories**
Hoover	1930s	Great Depression

Audrain County Time Line

	1932	Hardin College closes
	1934	Tom Bass dies
1933–45	**1936**	**Audrain Centennial**
F.D.Roosevelt		
	1937	**A.P.Green Fire Brick Co. world's largest**
	1940	S.P.Locke's *Warm Morning Stove*
1945–49	1941	Pearl Harbor; World War II
(Truman)		Congressional Medal of Honor to **S.G.Fuqua** of Laddonia
	1948	KXEO on air
	1949	Community R-VI School District
1949–53	1950	**Third Courthouse**
Truman		Mexico featured in LIFE magazine
		Korean War
	1950-64	**F.B.Hollingsworth** (Dem.)to Missouri Supreme Court
	1951	Highway R-III School District
1953–61	1954	Integration in schools
Eisenhower		
	1956	Van-Far School District
1961–63		
Kennedy	1966	1st Republican to County Court: Peter Todsen
1963–65		KWWR-FM on air
(L.Johnson)		See TV
1965–69	1968	Hart Vo.-Tech. School
Johnson		Vietnam War
	1970	**Audrain Medical Center**
		Miss Missouri Pageant to Mexico
1969–74	1973	**C.S.Bond** (Rep.) Governor of Missouri, 1st Term
Nixon		
1974–77	1977	1st Republican Circuit Judge: E.D.Hodge
(Ford)	1981	**C.S.Bond** (Rep.) Governor of Missouri, 2nd Term
1977–81	1985	MMA Honored by President Reagan
Carter	**1986**	**Audrain Sesquicentennial**
1981–89		Sale of *Ledger* by White
Reagan	1987	**C.S.Bond** (Rep.) to U.S. Senate

Leta Hodge

About the Author

$\mathbb{L}$ eta Tucker Hodge was born in 1934 in Tientsin, China, where her father was in business. Her childhood years, interrupted by war, were spent in Shanghai and in LaCrosse and Chester, Virginia, where she graduated from high school in 1952.

She attended Westhampton College, University of Richmond, graduating Phi Beta Kappa in 1956 with a B.A. degree in history.

After teaching history in high school she returned to academic pursuits, in 1959 receiving a Woodrow Wilson Fellowship and the following year a Thomas Jefferson Fellowship for graduate study at the University of Virginia. Her field of concentration is nineteenth-century social and cultural American history.

She moved to Mexico in 1961, where her husband practiced law before becoming circuit judge.

In 1980 she became director of the Audrain County Historical Society, serving until 1990. She has taught an adult education class on local history and has written articles on Mexico and Audrain County.

She is the author of *Soldiers, Scholars, Gentlemen: The First Hundred Years of the Missouri Military Academy; The Friend of Audrain: A History of Medicine in Audrain County;* and *A Legacy of Faith: The Story of the First Presbyterian Church of Mexico, Missouri.*

The publication of this book was made possible by a grant from the

Allen P. and Josephine B. Green Foundation

The Audrain County Historical Society and the author deeply appreciate their generosity and this recognition of the importance of preserving our local heritage.